Language matters

Donna Jo Napoli

Language matters

A guide to everyday questions about language

OXFORD
UNIVERSITY PRESS

2003

OXFORD
UNIVERSITY PRESS

Oxford   New York

Auckland   Bangkok   Buenos Aires   Cape Town   Chennai
Dar es Salaam   Delhi   Hong Kong   Istanbul   Karachi   Kolkata
Kuala Lumpur   Madrid   Melbourne   Mexico City   Mumbai   Nairobi
São Paulo   Shanghai   Taipei   Tokyo   Toronto

Copyright © 2003 by Oxford University Press

Published by Oxford University Press, Inc.
198 Madison Avenue, New York, New York 10016

www.oup.com

Oxford is a registered trademark of Oxford University Press

Library of Congress Cataloging-in-Publication Data
Napoli, Donna Jo, 1948-
Language matters : a guide to everyday questions about language /
Donna Jo Napoli.
p. cm.
Includes bibliographical references.
ISBN 0-19-515528-9; ISBN 0-19-516048-7 (pbk.)
1. Language and languages—Miscellanea.   I. Title.
P107 .N37 2003
400—dc21   2002075810

The illustrations appearing on page 158 are from *The World's Writing System*,
edited by Peter T. Daniels and William Bright. Copyright 1996 by Oxford
University Press, Inc. Used by permission.

9 8 7 6 5 4 3 2

Printed in the United States of America
on acid-free paper

Preface

I've been teaching linguistics since 1973. Newspaper and magazine reporters approach me in that role with questions—ranging all over the board—that often reveal misconceptions about language. We use language in most of our daily interactions with other people, so the types of questions that can arise are at least as varied as the types of situations in which we use language. Here are some examples:

> How can we stop our children from using bad grammar?
> Why don't we reform English spelling so that the words will be spelled exactly as we all say them?
> Isn't it interesting that the Inuit have dozens of words for snow when Americans can't even imagine all those different varieties?

The first question is problematic because the whole notion of good versus bad grammar is problematic. How do we decide whose grammar is good and whose is not? Language changes from one generation to the next, no matter what, and change is simply that—neither improvement nor decline; it is merely change. The second question is based on the assumption that we all pronounce words in the same way. Even within the United States that is false, but certainly, when we look at Canada, England, India, Australia, and other countries where English is one of the national languages, the falsity of that assumption is obvious. The third question is based on false information: So far as I know, it has never been determined whether or not the Inuit people have dozens of words for snow. Moreover, any active skier in the United States can rattle off descriptions (maybe using multiple words) of many different kinds of snow quality—so we can certainly understand concepts without having single-word labels for them.

When I respond to reporters' questions, sometimes my knowledge of particular languages and of the formal nature of linguistic principles helps me. This is particularly true if their questions are about how language is produced and processed or about particular sociolinguistic facts, such as differences between regional speech patterns. But I am struck by how often these questions could have been answered by anybody who took the time to seriously consider language use. Ordinary speakers have a great deal of knowledge about language, and if they apply common sense in analyzing language, they can debunk many common misconceptions.

Most people, however, have little idea of how to approach language questions. If you want to learn about language in a formal way, I encourage you to pick up a linguistics textbook or to take a linguistics course. But if you want to learn how to look at language issues so that you can make sensible and responsible decisions about language in your daily life, then this book will help you.

The chapters in this book are divided into two parts. Part I deals with language as a human ability. Part II deals with language in the context of society. At the end of each chapter is a list of readings for further consultation, as well as websites that were available when this book was written (in spring 2002). Another wonderful resource is the website of videos on language set up by the Linguistic Society of America: http://www.uga.edu/lsava/Archive.html.

The chapters invite you into one way of approaching language. They help you to uncover assumptions behind language questions so that you can evaluate them. They help you to recognize what sorts of things might be evidence for or against different positions on a language issue. And they help sort out the evidence in a systematic and methodologically sound way. Although only a dozen issues are addressed in this book, I hope that reading these chapters will give you the confidence to approach other language issues in a systematic way.

The title of each chapter is in question form. I use questions that do not have misconceptions built into them so that readers will not have these false ideas chiseled into their memories. However, each chapter addresses one or more misconceptions.

Linguistics is a field in which reasonable people can and do disagree. Nevertheless, in this book I am rarely equivocal (I'm a linguist, not a politician). But the arguments are laid out step by step, so if you disagree at any point along the way, you can diverge and find your own answers, knowing, at least, what my position is and why.

Acknowledgments

Many people helped me in writing this book. All the reporters and students I've had over the years have influenced me, particularly my students at Swarthmore College in Linguistics 1 in spring 2001. Peter Ohlin, the linguistics editor for Oxford University Press, asked me if I would write this book, then went on to shepherd me through every step along the way. Several anonymous reviewers made wonderful suggestions about every aspect of the book. And I thank Sean Crist, Amy DiBenedetto, Lillie Dremeaux, Barry Furrow, Krista Gigone, Richard Tchen, Jeff Wu, and Chandra Yesiltas for reading drafts and making comments.

Contents

part I

Language: The Human Ability

1 How do we acquire language?

How did you and I learn to speak and understand language? This is a difficult question to approach because even though we've all done it, we can't remember doing it. Acquiring language begins in the womb, and our accessible memories don't go back that far.

Nevertheless, many of us might be willing to attempt an answer. After all, we acquired language, so we must know something about the process. But is this true? We metabolize sugar, but unless we've studied chemistry, we don't know how it's done. It happens naturally; the body does it on its own.

A common misconception is that children need to be taught language. In fact, though, acquiring language happens naturally— just like metabolizing sugar. No one has to teach us; our brain does it on its own. This chapter presents some of the important evidence.

Most of the time we can find evidence in our daily language experience that is relevant in evaluating hypotheses about how language works. One of the purposes of this book is to help you recognize that evidence. Therefore, I hesitate to draw on data that you don't have easy access to. But sometimes relatively inaccessible data can be amazingly helpful, and this is one of those times. We begin by looking at data that you couldn't be expected to have access to if you hadn't studied linguistics. Our goal will be to find out what factors are necessary and/or sufficient for language acquisition to take place.

Let's confront the idea that children need to be taught language in an explicit and conscious way. This is false. There are language communities in which no conscious language teaching goes on, but language acquisition proceeds normally. In Samoa, for example, adults do not view infants and small children as conversational partners, nor do they feel a responsibility to model their speech so that children can more easily learn it. Instead, the children simply overhear speech between adults. Likewise, the adults do not listen to the speech of the children. It's as though the children's talk is not part of the larger language community. Yet the children acquire the language of the larger community just fine and at the same rate that children acquire language all around the world. Conscious language teaching, then, is not necessary for first language acquisition.

A new possibility might come to you (as it often has to my students): Children in these communities must be learning solely by mimicking, so maybe mimicking is sufficient for language acquisition. That idea, however, is also wrong.

There have been instances in which children have grown to adolescence in (almost) complete linguistic deprivation. For example, there is a well-documented case about a child dubbed the Wild Boy of Averyon. In 1799 a feral boy was found living in the woods of Averyon in the south of France. His habits included eating off the floor and making noises that resembled canine sounds. All indications were that he had been raised by wild animals. Although Doctor Jean-Marc Itard, an educator who had much success in teaching speech to deaf children (the Wild Boy of Averyon was not deaf), put years of work into trying to teach him human language, he never acquired more than a small vocabulary, with no sign of a system of rules for putting those words together into sentences.

Another example involves a girl researchers called Genie, who was discovered in 1970 in Los Angeles, living in captive isolation that limited both her physical activity and linguistic input. At the time of her discovery, she could hardly walk and gave no indication of knowing what speech was. Several researchers worked for years to teach Genie language, but she never progressed beyond an unsystematic stringing together of a few words. In middle age, she stopped talking altogether, and researchers gave up.

There are other cases of children (often raised by depraved adults) who never acquired facility with language. Over and over again, adults (often researchers) taught these children to mimic, but mimicry did not result in language acquisition. Mimicry is not a sufficient means of acquiring language.

These are extreme cases. Most children, although not overtly corrected by their parents when they make linguistic mistakes, are exposed to a tremendous amount of language modeling. Also, most children do a lot of mimicry as part of the process of acquiring language. Nevertheless, overt teaching is not necessary and mimicry is not sufficient. Instead, something else is the crucial factor, and it turns out to be biology.

For a couple of decades a team of researchers in London and Oxford studied members of a British family who exhibited an inherited and rare language disorder. Finally, they found another child, not related, who exhibited the same severe disorder. This led to the discovery in 2001 of a gene, called FOXP2, that is directly involved in language ability. There is no doubt: Language is a biological matter, and humans diverged from chimps and other primate lineages in this regard approximately 4.6 to 6.2 million years ago.

For the past half century, linguists have hypothesized that there is a language mechanism in the brain, an actual physical mechanism, that is responsible for all aspects of language, including learning, processing, and production. This mechanism is probably physiologically discontinuous. That is, it is not a single whole, like a kidney, liver, or other major organ. Instead, various parts of the language mechanism are located in separate spots in the brain and they work together to produce comprehensive language ability. The failure of the Wild Boy of Aveyron and of Genie to acquire language is taken as evidence that the language mechanism somehow changes at an early age, perhaps the age of five (although who knows for sure, since we cannot ethically do experiments), so the ability to acquire a first language after that critical period is diminished or even erased.

Further evidence for the existence of the language mechanism comes from data on linguistic damage and language pathologies. It's commonly known that strokes can result in severe language loss in a person whose intelligence is otherwise left intact. There are also several other types of damage to the brain that cause particular language impairments, and, significantly, if the site of the damage is known, the symptoms are predictable. For example, damage to the front part of the brain's left hemisphere results in the loss of the ability to use a coherent word order and general sentence structure. The afflicted person produces short and choppy utterances and exhibits a general lack of fluency. This condition is known as Broca's aphasia. Damage to the rear part of the brain's left hemisphere results in the loss of the ability to use words appropriate to meaning, to interpret language, or both. It is known as Wernicke's aphasia. Damage to the brain's entire left hemisphere results in all of these malfunctions and is known as global aphasia. In such instances, damage has been done to different parts of the language mechanism.

Also, there are pathologies linked to congenital problems. For example, children born with spina bifida sometimes experience devastating retardation. Nevertheless, they can articulately recount imagined events (events that never occurred), sounding entirely of normal intelligence when they do so. Here the language mechanism clearly operates independently of the damaged intelligence.

Some children are born with a set of syndromes that have been called Specific Language Impairment. These children do not have abnormal intelligence or any kind of sensory or emotional, social, or behavioral problems. Their problems are concentrated specifically on language issues; they have trouble understanding language and producing well-formed sentences. Again, the language mechanism has a pathology independent of any other brain function.

Once we've concluded that a language mechanism exists in the brain as a physical entity and that it changes over time, the question of how we acquire a first language is similar to the question of how we metabolize sugar in that any biological function has to be studied scientifically to be understood.

I'm now going to present data I have collected on first language acquisition. Some of these data are rather ordinary, but others I sought out to make my point. Although the data are largely anecdotal, in every instance there are studies, based on large data corpuses, that show that these cases are representative of ordinary language acquisition (unless I explicitly say otherwise).

Let's start with newborns. Here's the first scene: A baby fresh from the hospital is in his grandmother's arms, crying continuously. The grandmother, who has flown in from Florida for the occasion, is singing and cooing and cuddling the newborn to her breast. The mother comes through the door and coos as she crosses the room. At the first sound of her voice, the baby's cries turn to gulps that cease by the time the mother reaches him. What is the baby responding to? When the mother first came through the door, she was too far away for him to smell her, and the grandmother is holding him in such a way that his eyes can take in only his grandmother's face and chest. It appears that this newborn recognizes his mother's voice.

At the beginning of this chapter, I claimed that language acquisition starts in the womb. Around the seventh month of gestation, the auditory system is formed and, except in an instance of hearing impairment, functions well enough that fetuses can listen to the world outside the womb. It's not surprising, then, that a (hearing) newborn comes into the world recognizing the voices of his mother and of those people who constantly surround his mother. Surely the newborn is not consciously trying to acquire language. He simply listens to the world, yet already he has learned to pick out certain sounds as relevant to his various needs and wants.

Here's a second scene: I gave a talk to a social club of Korean women living in Ann Arbor, Michigan, all of whom sent their children to Korean school on Saturday to keep the language alive among their children. After the talk, my husband came in with our four-month-old son. I put Robert in the arms of one of the Korean women and went to the refreshments area for sandwiches. The women exclaimed over Robert in Korean. There was a constant coming and going of women who were peeking into his face and touching his hair and back. He gazed around happily, his eyes going from the women to the furniture to the lights (he loved lights). Then I whispered to a food server to please go over and say something, pretty much anything, to Robert. She did. And when he heard her speak, he turned to her immediately and gave her a giant smile and started to babble. She spoke English, her native language, which is the language Robert heard at home.

To conclude that Robert could distinguish English from Korean might seem rash, given this one instance. But studies on children as young as Robert show that English-speaking children can pick out English from French and other languages, just as French-speaking children can pick out French from English and other languages. In these studies the children's recognition of English is indicated by increased eye activity and heartbeat, rather than the smile and babbling that Robert produced, but the studies were done under laboratory conditions, whereas Robert's situation was a social one. So by very early in the first year of life, children have somehow managed to separate, from all the various noises they encounter, not just speech sounds but also the speech sounds of their own, native language. They are on the road to acquiring the sound system of their language.

Here's a third scene: A mother carries her ten-month-old into the child's bedroom. She says, "Want to turn on the light, Maggie? Go on. Press." Maggie's mouth opens and she twists in her mother's arms and presses the wall switch. The overhead light goes on. "La," says Maggie. "That's right," says her mother, "You turned on the light. You're such a smart girl."

Maggie picked out the word "light" from the stream of her mother's talk. If you look at that stream, it's rather complicated. This mother did not use any of the special devices that some people use when talking with babies—so-called "motherese." So she didn't say, for example, "Baby turn on light? Light light. See the light?" where the very preponderance of the utterance "light" could have been a clue. Instead, the mother talked to her baby daughter in ordinary language. Nevertheless, Maggie processed the speech well enough to know what to do. And, in fact, studies have shown that children exposed to ordinary talk acquire speech at the same rate as those exposed to large amounts of motherese.

You may object to my analysis, saying that this scene doesn't show that Maggie picked out the word "light" since turning on the light is probably part of the night-time routine. Maggie is primed not just by the word "light" but also by all the other factors that mark this routine (she's just had her bath and they're going into the bedroom). Maybe if the mother hadn't said anything, Maggie would have still reached around and turned on the light.

So I encourage you to test that hypothesis. Find a child like Maggie who likes to turn on lights. Then hold the child and stand near a wall switch, but with your back to it, so that you aren't making the task obvious. Ask the child to turn on the light. I can't guess what the child will do, but the point is that you can test your hypothesis. If you're going to take a scientific approach to the question of how we learn language, you need to come up with testable hypotheses and actually test them.

What is undeniable is that children do learn to pick out individual words. The literature on first language acquisition points to the first birthday as a time when most children start to produce words. Then at some point during their second year, they move into a two-word phase, in which one word refers to an object and the other word operates on the object in some way. Typical utterances are these:

More grape.
All gone.
Daddy shoe.
Doggy good.

Sometime around the child's third birthday, give or take six months, language takes a giant leap, and children start producing long sentences with varying degrees of morphological and syntactic complexity. Typical utterances at this stage are these:

What that girl doing? She get hurt.
I wrote this. See?
Time to go. Put your shoes on. We got to hurry.
Let me do it, me, don't help.
You can't talk. No. Don't talk.
Eva cry. Somebody hurt Eva.

Some utterances can be much more complex. My oldest daughter was two years and seven months old when her brother was born. Two weeks after his birth, she climbed into the center of my husband's and my bed and said:

Nobody doesn't love me no more.

When my oldest son was two years and four months, he came running in from the backyard, saying:

Oh, Mamma, somebody made cacca in my pants.

By this point (two years old) children can produce literally thousands of words, and by the time they are four years old they will have acquired all the elements of language, though their mastery of details can take many more years.

All the generalizations I have reported to you about the one-word phase, the two-word phase, and eventual sentences come from the literature on first language acquisition. In my own family experience, with five children, some of the generalizations I reported do not hold. Both my husband and I always spoke to our children in ordinary language. We spoke to them a lot, as well as read to them and sang to them. Two of our children started producing single words around the age of nine months, one started at six months, and another said almost nothing until she was two. Then one day as we were reading a book together, she pointed at a butterfly and said, "Bubbafwy." I was so excited, I called the family together and asked Eva to say it again, but she smiled at me and remained silent. She really didn't say much else until she turned three, at which point she went from single-word utterances to two-word utterances to constant (and I mean incessant) chattering in the span of about a month. My middle child acquired language in a way that confounded me entirely. I'd say, "What would you like to drink, Nick?" And he'd answer, "Awamih," with an intonation drop on the last syllable. Then he'd reach for the milk. One day when he was one year and five months old, I decided to try to help him learn in an explicit way. So I said, "Nick, you have to say 'milk' if you want milk." Nick looked at me earnestly and said vehemently, "Awamih." I said slowly and loudly, "Milk. You have to say 'milk.'" Nick said slowly and loudly, "Awamih." That's when I finally got it. He was saying, "I want milk," a whole sentence, not just a single word. His intonation should have told me that all along. Nick never went through the one-word or two-word phase. He simply spoke in sentences, sentences that were extremely hard for me to catch since his mastery of the sound system of English was typical for his age. Until he was around two, most people outside the family didn't know what he was saying, but we, at least, finally understood.

My point here is not to say that the researchers are wrong but that acquiring language, like gaining the skills of walking or running or skipping, occurs in different ways with different children. There may be a canonical pattern that we can all point to, but the fact remains that we (as individuals) might not know a single given child who actually went through the exact stages reported in the literature during the exact time periods predicted, despite the fact that the statistics can be verified in repeated experiments.

So how is it all happening? Consider the utterance, "More grape." This was said as a request at lunch. Notice that the child didn't say, "Grape more." Word order is well in place in this child's utterance, as in all the two-word utterances above. Go out and listen to children. They rarely scramble words, although they are exposed to many words in various orders in different sentences. The child may even have been exposed to these exact words in the opposite order. Consider these sentences:

I like **grape more** than orange.
He's **gone all** the time.
This is the **shoe Daddy** fixed.
What a **good doggy**.

The boldfaced words are in reverse order from the children's two-word utterances given above. So the word order the children use cannot be due simply to exposure. Somehow children are fitting words into the proper order for the meaning that they want—proper with respect to their native language. A child who speaks a language that has operators that follow the objects they operate on (such as a language in which the verb follows the object, giving something like "book read" instead of "read book"), for example, will use the opposite word order from that of a child who speaks English. In other words, children arrange their words according to abstract linguistic principles, principles no one explicitly teaches them.

Likewise, whereas children's early utterances are often brief, they have structure. Thus, corresponding to the adult utterance

When are you coming?

the child might say:

When?

or

When come?

but would never say

Are?

or

When you?

The child's utterance is not simply a truncation of the adult's. It has a grammar, and that grammar gradually develops into the adult grammar.

In fact, many children are exposed to ungrammatical language, yet they produce grammatical language. Consider, for example, a situation that many of us have witnessed: children of immigrants who have at best only a rudimentary knowledge of English. These children hear their parents saying such sentences as "Paper no come today," but the children produce, "The paper didn't come today." Instead of mimicking their parents (who might even be making a word-for-word translation from their native language into English), these children use the language they hear in the world outside the family. They glean the linguistic rules of English from sentences spoken by native speakers, who have a coherent grammar, not those spoken by their parents, who might well have an incoherent grammar in English.

Even more striking facts hold in a situation that most of us have probably not witnessed: children of parents who speak a pidgin— a language put together piecemeal by adults of varying languages who are thrown together and must communicate however they can. These children hear utterances that do not conform to recognizable principles of natural language grammar, yet they produce utterances that do conform to such principles: they speak a creole language. (Both pidgins and creoles are discussed in chapter 8.) Once more, it's clear that children are using principles that must be encoded somehow in the language mechanism—principles of natural language that are fundamental and thus form what linguists call Universal Grammar, or UG.

Finally, consider the case of cryptophasia (secret languages), often used at home. Many children, when left with other children for long periods, will develop special ways of talking together. This is quite common, although for most children the game of creating a language loses its attraction fairly quickly, so the secret language is abandoned before it might become fully formed. Sometimes, however, the language blossoms. There are studies of such languages between twins, called twin language, and there have been studies of such sign languages within a family, called home sign. Significantly, twin languages and home sign exhibit natural grammars; they conform to UG. In the twin cases, the twins also speak a community language, so one might argue that the UG characteristics of twin language are carried over from the community language. However, in some of the instances of home sign, the child signers, at least, do not participate in any other community language but do not introduce nonnatural elements into their signs. Thus language created by children conforms to UG even when the children have no access to any community language.

We are hard-wired to process and produce natural human language. We acquire our specific native language in a natural way, by sifting through what we are exposed to or what we create with the UG principles that we are born with. The data presented here from other cultures and those on linguistically deprived children and on the biology of language all make this point. But, importantly, we could arrive at this conclusion on our own, without these rather esoteric data, by looking scientifically at examples of children's language. Methodical study of relevant language data can take us a long way.

Further Readings

Berwick, R. 1985. *The acquisition of syntactic knowledge.* Cambridge, Mass.: MIT Press.

Brown, R. 1973. *A first language: The early stages.* Cambridge, Mass.: Harvard University Press.

Chomsky, N. 1975. *Reflections on language.* New York: Random House.

Clark, E. 1993. *The lexicon in acquisition*. New York: Cambridge University Press.

Heath, S. 1983. *Ways with words: Language, life, and work in communities and classrooms*. New York: Cambridge University Press.

Ingram, D. 1989. *First language acquisition: Method, description, and explanation*. New York: Cambridge University Press.

Lai, C., S. Fisher, J. Hurst, F. Vargha-Khadems, and A. Monaco. 2001. A forkhead-domain gene is mutated in severe speech and language disorder. *Nature*, 413: 519–23.

Locke, J. 1993. *The child's path to spoken language*. Cambridge, Mass.: Harvard University Press.

Pinker, S. 1984. *Language learnability and language development*. Cambridge, Mass.: Harvard University Press.

———. 1994. *The language instinct*. New York: Morrow.

Slobin, D., ed. 1985–1992. *The crosslinguistic study of language acquisition*. 3 vols. Hillsdale, N.J.: Erlbaum.

Wexler, K., and P. Culicover. 1980. *Formal principles of language acquisition*. Cambridge, Mass.: MIT Press.

Web Sites

Cornell University. 1997. *Papers on language acquisition: Cornell working papers in linguistics*, vol. 15, http://www.clal.cornell.edu/lab/publications/working_papers.htm

Deysher, S. Study investigates children's development of sentence processing mechanisms. http://www.cis.upenn.edu/~ircs/current_topics/eyetracker/story.html

Language acquisition. http://www.facstaff.bucknell.edu/rbeard/acquisition.html

Pinker, S. Language acquisition. http://www.cogsci.soton.ac.uk/~harnad/Papers/Py104/pinker.langacq.html

2

From one language to the next:
Why is it hard to learn a second language?
Why is translation so difficult?

In the first chapter we looked at first language acquisition. There are important differences between acquiring a first language—a process that happens naturally to any child who is not linguistically deprived—and learning a second. The use of "acquiring" in one case and "learning" in the other is not accidental. Scholars debate, in fact, whether or not the cognitive faculties that are employed in second language learning are distinct from those employed in first language acquisition, and most of the evidence suggests that they are.

First, anyone who is learning a second language has already acquired a first language, so the language mechanism in the brain already has had certain linguistic parameters (such as word order) set, making the task quite different. What needs to be learned are the specific rules of the second language—often called the target language. The first language typically serves as the model, and errors often result from taking words from the target language and stringing them together by applying rules from the first language. So, for example, if the first language is English and the target language is Japanese, a second language learner might position the Japanese verb between the subject and the object of the sentence, using the English word order, rather than placing the verb after the object, which is the correct Japanese word order. The greater the difference between the first language and the target language, the more tasks are involved in learning the latter. Second language learning can even be characterized as a gradual shift from the first language orientation to the target language orientation.

Second, first language acquisition takes place in early childhood (by the age of five usually) and, typically, cannot take place after that critical period. But second language learning, especially in a classroom setting, proceeds more quickly with adults and adolescents than with younger children initially, although ultimately the younger child will become more proficient in the second language than the adolescent or adult. That is, second language learning proceeds more quickly with people who have a high proficiency in their first language.

Third, whereas first language acquisition happens without conscious teaching, second language learning generally does not. Thus the process is distinct. Studies have shown that self-confidence, motivation, good self-image, and low anxiety are traits that improve facility in a second language, but none of these traits is important to first language acquisition.

Fourth, the complexity of input affects second language learning but not first language acquisition. For example, if a second language learner has a classroom teacher who talks in the target language at a quick rate, in complex sentences, and about complicated matters, the learner will have a harder time initially than if simpler constructions are presented about matters that don't involve a lot of decision making or mental judgment. But first language acquisition proceeds at the same rate whether or not adults simplify their language.

Fifth, practice is important for second language learning but not so much for first language acquisition. Even very quiet children, who are reticent to talk, acquire first language at the ordinary rate.

The two processes have some things in common, however. Second language learning proceeds more quickly if the target language is used as the medium of instruction. So exposure to ordinary speech is important, just as it is in first language acquisition, although it can help if that speech is a little bit slower and less complex initially. In fact, second language learning is more successful when richly interactive language is used in the classroom. Instructional conversations are better teaching tools than memorization drills or lectures and recitations. And certainly conversations are more like the ordinary language one is exposed to in first language acquisition than are memorization drills and the like.

So far I've presented several generalizations that you can find in the literature on second language learning, and I haven't introduced any controversy. In chapter 11, we will try to put ourselves in one situation that some second language learners face. But that chapter is mainly about language policy, and it doesn't deal extensively with the kinds of questions posed to people who are learning a second language. Here, I want to look at precisely those kinds of questions. We will do so by turning to the issue of translation, which allows us rather quickly to wrestle with a wide range of issues relevant to second language learning.

One Italian saying is "Traduttori traditori," which is translated word for word as "translators traitors." The idea is that translation can never be perfect, so anyone who translates necessarily betrays the original.

Various types of activities fall under the rubric of "translation." The Certificate of Foreign Status of Beneficial Owner for United States Tax Withholding form (federal tax document form W-8BEN) asks in Part 1, line 1, for "Name of individual or organization that is the beneficial owner." When a recent Norwegian visitor to my college read this phrase aloud and asked what it meant, the administrative assistant said, "Let me translate: 'you.'" Here the word "translate" was used to refer to an explanation through re-wording within a language (intralingual translation).

Another way in which the word "translation" is used can be seen in the following situation. One of my college students wrote a poem, and another one did a dance that she called a "translation" of the poem. Here the word refers to an interpretation of one medium in another (intersemiotic translation).

I want to restrict the discussion to a third sense of "translation," the most common and the one most relevant to second language learning—interpreting from one human language into another human language, the activity the Italian saying claims is impossible to do with total accuracy (interlingual translation). Is the saying right? Or is true translation possible?

Students in high school language classes are continually asked to translate between languages. Probably you've been asked to do that, and you might even be able to remember some of the questions you faced. But rather than make a list of the types of potential issues that come up, let's just jump into a translation exercise together.

We could choose a variety of texts to translate, for some of which the only real job is to transmit factual information grammatically. Think of translating legal documents, driving directions, or instructions on how to construct a harpsichord from a kit. Translating such texts is a matter of strict adherence to the (perceived) intended informational message of the original author. The translator can easily ignore the style of the original text without much threat of criticism. Instead of any of these types of texts, though, I'm going to choose poetry because the range of factors to consider is wider and because true facility in a second language entails recognition of these factors.

There are various types of poetry translations. Some of them are similar to the approach used in translating factual texts, such as instructions, in that they do not consider all the factors present in the original. Let's look at an extreme case. The Austrian poet Ernst Jandl (1925–2000) focused on the importance of sound in poetry. He developed the art of "surface translation," whereby the sounds of a poem in one language would be rendered into another—using words native to the target language or nonsense words in the target language—without regard to meaning. When the two languages differ in their sound inventories (as most languages do), the closest approximation is acceptable. Here is an example of a poem in German by Rainer Maria Rilke, shown next to Jandl's surface translation into English. I've also provided a word-by-word translation, so you can see how the surface translation disregards the meaning of the words in the original poem.

Rilke's poem	*Surface translation*	*Word-by-word*
Der Tod ist gross.	Dare toadies gross	the death is big
Wir sind die Seinen	Vere sinned designing	we are the their
Lachenden Munds.	Laugh in the moons.	laughing mouths
Wenn wir uns mitten	When we've ounce mitten	when we us middle
im Leben meinen	Am lay-by mine in-	in life mine
wagt er zu weinen	Farct hair so whining	wake he to crying
mitten in uns.	Midden in noons.	middle in us

I am not going to deal with surface translation of this sort but rather with holistic translation, which is more pertinent to second language learning.

Let's start by trying to translate a poem into English from a language that is quite similar to English—Dutch. Annette Hoeksema gave me this nursery rhyme, which Dutch children enjoy, and she translated each word individually for me:

Leentje leerde Lotje lopen
In de lange Lindenlaan
Maar toen Lotje niet wou lopen
Liet Leentje Lotje staan.

The very first word, *Leentje*, is a girl's name, as is the third word, *Lotje*. Do we leave them as is (in the Dutch), on the grounds that names can carry over from one language to another? That is, do you call your Italian friend Giuseppe and your Israeli friend Leila? Or should we choose English names, in the way in which you might call your Italian friend Joe and your Israeli friend Lilly?

The question may seem trivial, but it isn't. Our choice here might elicit emotional responses from the reader that we must be sensitive to. Let's say you have an Italian friend named Graziella. Do you call her Graziella or Grace? If you live in a city, probably neither choice seems very strange to you, and you'd be happy enough calling her Graziella. If you live in a small rural town, however, one where immigrants haven't been seen for generations, "Graziella" might seem to be a rather exotic name, one that could tend to isolate her from the community and one that you might even feel pretentious saying. We are trying to translate a nursery rhyme together, so maybe we want to stay away from anything that isolates the protagonists in the rhyme from the children who are reciting it and from anything that smacks of pretension.

All right, then, on the grounds that I want unpretentious names, I'm going to translate *Leentje* as "Little Linda" and *Lotje* as "Lottie." You might object that in Dutch *Leentje* and *Lotje* both end in *tje*. So maybe these two names have something in common that should be preserved when we translate them. If you made this objection, you'd be right—*-tje* is a diminutive ending, comparable to the "-y" in "Johnny" and the "-ie" in "Bessie." If we put the word "little" with one name but use the English diminutive "-ie" with the other, we lose this similarity between the names. So do we say "Lindy" and "Lottie" or "Little Linda" and "Little Lottie"? One problem with the second choice is that the diminutive is already present in "Lottie," so having "little" as well seems unnecessary. On the other hand, maybe in your experience "Lindy" is unusual, making the first choice feel too exotic for a nursery rhyme. You might even want to substitute "Lindsay" for "Lindy."

How did we get into all this trouble just dealing with something so straightforward as proper names? Since there are many other issues for us to resolve, I'm simply going to translate the names as "Lindy" and "Lottie" and forge ahead.

Let's go to the other words in the first line: *leerde* means "taught" (it is marked for the past tense and for agreement with a third-person singular subject) and *lopen* is the infinitive (the completely tenseless form that has no agreement) for the verb "walk." We can now translate the first line, word for word:

Lindy taught Lottie walk

This isn't a grammatical sentence in English. I chose Dutch to start our investigation because it is so similar to English that word-by-word translations often yield grammatical results. I wanted our attempt at translation to be successful. We've hit a glitch here, though. The problem is with the verb "teach." Several other verbs would have yielded a good sentence, for example:

Lindy {helped/let/made/watched/heard/saw} Lottie walk

However, for "teach" we need the extra word "to" in front of the verb "walk." So let's translate the four words in line 1 of the Dutch nursery rhyme with an English line that consists of five words:

Lindy taught Lottie to walk

(Notice that many verbs behave like "teach" in requiring "to" before a following infinitive verb.)

Now let's go to the words in the second line: *In* means "in," *de* means "the," and *lange* means "long." The last word, *Lindenlaan*, is a proper name again, the name of a road. *Linden* has to do with linden trees, and *-laan* is translated as (and historically related to) our word "lane." So let's say:

In the long Linden Lane

This has a fine sound to my ear (and it's because of how nicely Dutch translates into English that I chose it).

Let's move on to line 3. *Maar* means "but," *toen* means "then," *niet* means "not," *wou* means "wanted" (again, past tense, third person), and *lopen* (again) means "walk." If we translate word for word, we'll get

But then Lottie not wanted walk

Again, the result is ungrammatical in English. English requires that "to" precede the infinitive verb "walk," just as in line 1. English also requires another extra word because the negative "not" calls for an accompanying helping verb (This did not used to be so, however; compare the biblical "Judge not lest ye be judged" to ordinary modern talk.) So let's put in the appropriate form of "do":

But then Lottie did not want to walk

Read this line aloud. It's grammatical but stilted. In ordinary conversation we'd say "didn't" rather than "did not." So maybe the line should be

But then Lottie didn't want to walk

What can help us choose between these alternatives? Probably a consideration of our entire translation—the whole rhyme. But for now let's take the line with the contraction (the ordinary line), and you can reevaluate later if you want.

In the final line, *Liet* means "let" (past tense, third person, as with *leerde* and *wou*) and *staan* is the infinitive for "stand." A word-by-word translation yields

Let Lindy Lottie stand

Trouble again: Do you even know what this line means? "Lindy" is the subject of the sentence here, so in English we'd rearrange the words to get

Lindy let Lottie stand

Here's the first draft of our translation:

Lindy taught Lottie to walk
In the long Linden Lane
But then Lottie didn't want to walk
Lindy let Lottie stand

We are not done yet. Since this is a nursery rhyme in Dutch, we want it to be a nursery rhyme in English. Therefore, we need to see whether our translation has the characteristic elements of an English nursery rhyme. Nursery rhymes are often recognizable by their sound. Say our first draft aloud. Try to say the Dutch lines aloud (even though you are unsure of how to pronounce them). Does our draft sound as much like a nursery rhyme as the Dutch does?

What are the sound elements of a nursery rhyme in English? One of them is rhyme itself. Dutch has a similar tradition. In the

Dutch, the odd lines rhyme (actually, they end in the same word), as do the even lines. In our translation, the odd lines rhyme (and they end in the same word), but the even ones don't. So the English is a little off here.

Another sound element of nursery rhymes in English is the rhythm. Since most of my readers probably don't know Dutch (nor do I), you're going to have to believe me on this point: When Annette said the poem for me, each line had four strong beats (i.e., four obviously stressed syllables). The number of weak beats in each line, on the other hand, varied. The rules of rhythm in Dutch nursery rhymes, then, are a lot like those in English nursery rhymes. Consider this:

Thìrty dàys hàth Septèmber
Àpril Jùne ànd Novèmber

(Note that there is a strong beat on the first syllable of "April.") The rule here is four strong beats to a line, but the number of weak beats doesn't matter. What kind of rhythmic pattern does our first draft of the translation have? A lot depends on how you say it aloud. As I read it, it has three strong beats in each line.

Lìndy taught Lòttie to wàlk
In the lòng Lìnden Làne
But then Lòttie didn't wànt to wàlk
Lìndy let Lòttie stànd

Shall we try to revise our translation to deal with these discrepancies? Let's take them one at a time. Certainly rhyme matters. So let's try to revise the nursery rhyme so that lines 2 and 4 rhyme, without losing the rhyme (here, identity) in lines 1 and 3. I began by trying to find words that rhyme with "lane," looking for one that would have a sense appropriate to the fourth line. I thought of "refrain," not a word you'd expect in a nursery rhyme. No happy fit comes to my mind.

We could give up on keeping "lane" and look for two words that rhyme, one that is similar in meaning to "lane" and one that is similar in meaning to "stand." I came up with "way" and "stay." If we accept the rhyme "way"/"stay," we give up the word "lane." Does that bother you? Notice how many of the words in the Dutch poem begin with the letter "l." This alliteration will be reduced if we replace "lane" with "way." On the other hand, *laan* in Dutch is not at the beginning of a word but rather is the second part of a compound word. So losing this alliteration is not so bad (perhaps), and now we will have a "w" alliteration, with the two instances of "walk." Therefore, I vote for the "way"/"stay" rhyme.

Next, consider the rhythm. The Dutch line has one more strong beat than the English line. Do we want to make the English line longer, perhaps? Or is this discrepancy acceptable? We have to be careful here because if we make the English line longer, we'll add words that don't correspond to anything in the Dutch line. On that basis alone, I vote to allow the discrepancy in rhythm.

One final point: To my ear, the English last line sounds abrupt, whereas to Annette's ear, the Dutch last line does not. I have opted, therefore, to add "so" at the beginning of the final line.

Now, let's look at the revision:

Lindy taught Lottie to walk
In the long Linden Way
But then Lottie didn't want to walk
So Lindy let Lottie stay

Perhaps we could do better than this, but I think that we've dealt with the major issues that this nursery rhyme offers. It's apparent that even something as simple as a nursery rhyme—and even

translating between two languages as close as English and Dutch—
offers serious challenges to the translator: Should significant or
repeated elements of word structure (such as diminutives) be maintained? To what extent should the translation preserve elements
of sound such as rhythm, rhyme, and alliteration? To what extent
should the translation preserve style? At what point should con-
serving meaning be sacrificed and to what extent?

Let's look at translation from the other side—that is, a translation from English. Can you think of English utterances that
present problems for a translator? What about

John kicked the bucket.

This is an idiom: It has a literal reading (one in which John slammed
his foot against a bucket) and a figurative reading (one in which
John died). If "kicked the bucket" is not understood in the target
language as meaning "die," how can we translate it to preserve the
dual reading? Do we abandon kicking and buckets altogether and
look for some analogous idiom in the target language?

Another question comes up when we think about how to translate a sentence such as:

The dinner table was so festive, I expected him to serve
    turkey.

This is an English sentence, yet we know it is probably said by an
American rather than an Australian, Englishman, or South African. The turkey makes us think of the American Thanksgiving. It
has that connotation, that cultural import. If someone were to translate this sentence into Chinese, would that person use the Chinese
word for turkey or pick some other food that was associated with a
big family holiday in China? Certainly, the translator could do
either—and the choice might well depend on the purpose of the

translation. If this is part of a story about American life, the translator would probably use a more literal translation. If this is part of a story with a universal theme and if the setting of America is not important, the translator might feel comfortable in using a translation that was truer to the connotations of the sentence.

But how far do we go? What if we're dealing with allusions rather than connotations? If there is a reference to Shakespeare and we're translating into Italian, do we change it to a reference to Dante? If we're translating into Russian, do we change it to a reference to Pushkin?

Problems like idioms and connotations of certain vocabulary items and allusions come up regardless of the languages you are translating, and I'm sure you can think of many more. Consider translating a passage into English that refers to an act of conversation. Do we use "chat," "talk," "discuss," "converse," "debate," or something else to denote that act? Formality and tone and other matters of style come into play regardless of the languages.

In fact, style is such an important part of translation that sometimes styles develop in a language that are used only for translated materials. For example, medieval Arabic translations of ancient Greek philosophic texts were quite literal, often simply word-by-word translations. This style wasn't used for other texts. These stilted translations were then translated into Hebrew in the 1100s to 1300s, carrying that style with them. The result was a special style of Hebrew used only for translation.

This situation may seem strange at first, but think about the Bible. Many people object to modern renditions because they believe that the earlier ones were truer to the language of the era. But some scholars say that the earlier renditions were stilted, even for their times; in other words, they used a translation language rather than a smoothly flowing one. Ironically, the accuracy of a biblical translation is particularly thorny since the identity of the original manuscript is constantly under debate.

Sometimes problems come up between languages X and Y that wouldn't come up between languages X and Z. For example, the sentence

She has brothers

can be translated easily from English to Indonesian. But if we try to translate it into Sanskrit, say, we'd need to know whether she had two brothers or more than two. English makes the simple distinction of singular versus more than one (which is our plural), as do many languages, including Indonesian. But Sanskrit makes the three-way distinction between singular, dual (precisely two), and more than two (which is their plural), as do certain other languages. Grammatical differences between languages, then, can introduce questions for the translator—sometimes questions the translator can't answer. Perhaps the sentence above is in a passage that says nothing more about her brothers, so the translator does not know whether she has two or more than two. What should one do? If I were unable to confirm the precise information, I'd use the Sanskrit plural rather than the dual simply because the former is less precise (being any number greater than two). But I might, in fact, be wrong.

What all this means is that before we can do a holistic translation of a text, we have to analyze it: We have to break it down into all the components that make it precisely what it is. Then we have to make judgment calls about how to render those components in the target language. Moreover, the target language might have differences in grammar that confound the translation, or it might belong to a culture that is different from the culture of the original language community in ways that again confound the translation. This analysis and this juggling act between grammars and cultures are part of every act of holistic translation, regardless of the languages. Compromises must be made, and the genius of translation lies, at least in part, in which compromises are made and how.

Naturally, then, different people are going to translate the same text in different ways. Here are the first five lines of a Latin poem written around 62 B.C.E. by the famous poet Gaius Valerius Catullus. (You do not have to know any Latin to follow the brief discussion below.)

> Miser Catulle, desinas ineptire,
> et quod vides perisse perditum ducas.
> fulsere quondam candidi tibi soles,
> cum ventitabas quo puella ducebat
> amata nobis quantum amabitur nulla.

(The full text and a translation into Italian can be found at www.latine.net/autori/catullo/versioni/carmini/carmini-5-9.htm.) Elaine Allard, Joel Blecher, Mary Campbell, Mara Fortes, and Ross Hoffman (students in my Linguistics 1 course in spring 2001) gathered four English translations of this poem for our class to analyze. All are by reputable scholars of the classics whose translations are renowned. I'll give the first few lines of each here (the ones I judge to be translations of the first five lines of the Latin poem), with the name of the translator and the year of the translation (or if I don't know it, the life span of the author).

1. Thomas Campion: 1567–1620

> Harden now thy tyred hart, with more than flinty rage;
> Ne'er let her false teares henceforth thy constant griefe
>   asswage.

Once true happy dayes thou saw'st when shee stood firme
    and kinde,
Both as one then liv'd and held one eare, one tongue, one
    minde:

2. Peter Whigham: 1980

Break off
fallen Catullus
time to cut losses,
bright days shone once,
you followed a girl
here & there
loved as no other
perhaps
shall be loved,

3. Jacob Rabinowitz: 1991

Joyless Catullus, stop playing the fool. Give up what you see
    is lost.
Those were your clear seasons, the sun shone frank and
    bright,
when you used to go wherever your girlfriend led.
—I loved her. No-one will ever love a girl that much.

4. Charles Martin: 1993

Wretched Catullus! You have to stop this nonsense,
admit that what you see has ended is over!
Once there were days which shone for you with rare
    brightness,
when you would follow wherever your lady led you,
the one we once loved as we will love no other;

Please read through these four translations again, and do it aloud this time. All differ in their arrangement into lines: Only Martin's has five lines, like the original (and his full translation has nineteen lines, like the original, but none of the other translations do). All differ in patterns of repetition: Campion's, for example, has rhyming couplets whereas the other three have only scattered repetition, like the original (but never exactly like the original). And all clearly differ in vocabulary choice.

What about style? Rabinowitz's and Martin's are close in style, and it is interesting to note that they are contemporaneous. It would appear from just these four examples, then, that style may be more a matter of the time of the translator than an inherent characteristic of the original poem.

We can conclude, then, that translation is not a mechanical act; it doesn't proceed by any sort of simple algorithm. Rather, translation is a creative act. Some have even said that translating is rewriting. Different translators will offer different translations of the same text from language X into language Y, as we have seen. These different translations will have different strengths and drawbacks. Poetry involves meter, cadence, imagery, phrasing, and the personality of the voice of the poem, as we saw in all the translations of the Catullus poem. Without regard to the original, which translation did you enjoy the most? In my opinion, Rabinowitz offered a translation whose essense is the sharp edge of feeling, and I'm grateful for that. Does that mean that translations can be judged independently of the original? That they are perhaps as valuable as originals? Some would say yes. Is one more (nearly) right than another? Or are all imperfect? Is true translation impossible to achieve, as some have argued?

One of the major flaws in the argument against the existence of true translations is in the assumption that there is one correct way to interpret any text. Take something simple:

I love you.

This can be interpreted one way when a nurturing parent speaks to her child; another way when a parent is inducing guilt in her child; another way when a couple decides to marry; another way when that couple has been married for fifty years; another way when a prostitute says it to a stranger who's paying her to say it; another way when a teenager is trying to manipulate a girlfriend or boyfriend; another way when a child says it to a parent at the end of a long and wonderful day; and so on. If you and I went to a movie together and then discussed every line in the screenplay, we would undoubtedly have different interpretations of some of the lines— even though we both witnessed the same movie and were both aware of the contexts for all of them. We bring with us our experience about life and language when we interpret what we hear. Understanding language is a creative process.

So either we say it's impossible for us to truly understand each other even when we're speaking the same language, or we allow ourselves to enjoy the fluidity of our linguistic interactions—and thus to happily read all sorts of literature in translation. Furthermore, with this attitude we can study a second language with optimism. As speakers of a second language, we are constantly facing the issues that a translator encounters. This doesn't mean that we always need to be translating from our native tongue. If we become good enough at the second language, we will not consciously go through such an intermediate stage. What second language speakers share with the translator is the creative task of expressing something in the target language in a way that will be maximally effective.

Can we do it? Can we ever be proficient enough at a second language to express ourselves as effectively in it as in our native language? I know so many people who speak multiple languages magnificently well that I have to believe the answer is yes. But being equally effective does not mean being identical. Our experiences in one language community will always be different from our experiences in another language community, and our experiences play a role in how we express ourselves.

Further Readings

Bialystok, E., ed. 1991. *Language processing in bilingual children.* Cambridge: Cambridge University Press.

Brown, H. D. 1994. *Principles of language learning and teaching*, 2nd ed. Englewood Cliffs, N.J.: Prentice Hall Regents.

de Groot, A., and J. Kroll. 1997. *Tutorials in bilingualism: Psycholinguistic perspectives*, Hillsdale, N.J.: Lawrence Erlbaum.

Ellis, R. 1985. *Understanding second language acquisition.* Oxford: Oxford University Press.

———. 1994. *The study of second language acquisition.* Oxford: Oxford University Press.

Flynn, S., and W. O'Neil. 1988. *Linguistic theory in second language acquisition.* Dordrecht: Kluwer.

Gardner, R., and W. Lambert, eds. 1972. *Attitudes and motivation in second language learning.* Rowley, Mass.: Newbury House.

Hakuta, K. 1986. *Mirror of language: The debate on bilingualism.* New York: Basic Books.

Krashen, S. 1981. *Second language acquisition and second language learning.* Oxford: Pergamon.

McLaughlin, B. 1987. *Theories of second language learning.* London: Edward Arnold.

Schulte, R., and J. Biguenet, ed. 1992. *Theories of translation.* Chicago, Ill.: University of Chicago Press.

Skehan, P. 1989. *Individual differences in second-language learning.* London: Edward Arnold.

Tharp, R. G., and R. Gallimore. 1988. *Rousing minds to life: Teaching,*

learning, and school in social context. New York: Cambridge
University Press.

White, L. 1990. *Universal grammar and second language acquisition.*
Amsterdam: John Benjamins.

Web Sites

Age and the acquisition process. http://ponce.inter.edu/proyecto/in/
huma/age.html

Center for advanced research on language acquisition. http://carla
.acad.umn.edu/CARLA.html

Collier, V. Acquiring a second language for school. http://www.ncbe
.gwu.edu/ncbeubs/directions/04.htm

Epstein, S., S. Flynn, and G. Martohardjono. Second language
acquisition: Theoretical and experimental issues in contemporary
research. http://cogprint.ecs.soton.ac.uk/bbs/Archive/bbs.epstein
.html

Hu, J. A new information processing model of SLA and its implications in teaching ESL to adult learners. http://nlu.nl.edu/ace/
Resources/documents/ESL.html

Language acquisition. http://earthrenewal.org/secondlang.htm

An overview of second language acquisition. http://cls.coe.utk.edu/
lpm/esltoolkit/03acquisition.html

Stephen Karshen's theory of second language acquisition. http://
www.sk.com/br/sk-krash.html

Twyford, C. Age-related factors in second language acquisition. http://
www.ncbe.gwu.edu/ncbepubs/classics/focus/02bage.htm

Walqui, A., and E. West. Contextual factors in second language
acquisition. http://www.cal.org/ericcll/digest/0005contextual
.html

Further Reading on Translation

Bell, R., and C. Candin. 1991. *Translation and translating: Theory and
practice.* Boston: Addison Wesley Longman.

Hatim, B., and I. Mason. 1990. *Discourse and the translator*. New York: Longman.

Larson, M. 1999. *Meaning-based translation: A guide to cross-language equivalence*. Lanham, Md.: University Press of America.

Newmark, P. 1991. *About translation*. Clevedon, Eng.: Multilingual Matters.

Shuttleworth, M., and M. Cowie. 1997. *Dictionary of translation studies*. Manchester, Eng.: St. Jerome Publishing.

Web Sites on Translation

Translation Journal. http://accurapid.com/journal/
Translation, theory, and technology. http://www.ttt.org/

3 Does language equal thought?

An idea fundamental to cognitive science is that it may be possible to describe our thought processes through some representational system. Whether the appropriate representational system has properties similar to linguistic properties (such as observing similar principles) is an open question that scholars will no doubt be debating for years. Here, however, I'd like to address related questions, ones that I believe we can answer together: Do we think in language? Could we think without a language?

One way to interpret these questions is as follows: Does language construct a mental world that cognitively fences us in? This might well be a familiar question to you since it is frequently debated.

One can also interpret these questions in the most mundane way, the way people do when they say things such as "It's so noisy I can't hear myself think"—that is, asking whether human beings think in specific human languages. In other words, do people from Italy think in Italian? Or, given that the Italian language has many dialects, we could break down this basic question into multiple ones, such as these: Do Venetians think in Venetian? Do Neapolitans think in Napoletano? Likewise, do Indians, Australians, Canadians, Americans, and the British think in their own national varieties of English? We can get nicer: Do Bostonians and Atlantans and Philadelphians think in their urban varieties? With either interpretation, the rest of this chapter will aim to convince you that the answer to these questions is no.

I am first going to argue that thought does not require language by giving you instances of thought that couldn't possibly have been formulated in the brain in terms of language. The argument is a little long, so please keep that end point in sight.

Think about living with a toddler. Let me give you five scenarios that I've witnessed—three typical, two just plain wonderful—in which children did not use spoken or sign language. Then I will bring out their relevance, as a group, to the central question of this chapter.

1. A boy plows a plastic truck across frozen grass. Another boy comes over, watches for a while, and then throws a handful of dirt on the first boy. The first boy picks up his truck, takes it to the area behind the swing set, and resumes plowing there.
2. My grandniece is coloring vehemently, and she rips the paper with the crayon. She takes another piece of paper, tapes it over the rip, and continues coloring.
3. A girl in the grocery store reaches for candy at the checkout aisle. Her mother says she can't have it. The girl throws a tantrum. Her mother's cheeks flame, and she gives the girl the candy.
4. Some three-year-olds sit in a line at the edge of a swimming pool, all of them with their feet dangling in the water. A man is teaching them to swim. He takes the first child on one end of the line and dunks him. That boy laughs. The instructor lifts him out of the pool, and the boy goes to the other end of the line. The instructor does the same to the next child, working his way along the line. My daughter,

who is terrified of pools, is in the middle of the line. When the instructor lifts the third child, my daughter reaches both hands into the pool, splashes herself, then runs to the end of the line—with the children who have already been dunked.

5. A boy goes to the beach with his family. The family on the next blanket has a blind child. The two children start digging together. At one point the mother of the first boy calls him over for a snack of carrot sticks. The boy takes his bag to the other boy and holds it out for him. When the blind boy doesn't react, the first boy takes the blind boy's hand (so beautifully covered with sand) and sticks it in the plastic bag. They share sandy carrots.

All of these scenarios give evidence of reasoning on the part of the child and, thus, of thought. Perhaps you disagree with me about one or another, but surely you agree about at least one. Now we are almost ready to approach the question of the relationship of thought to language in these types of scenarios.

But first, let's approach one more situation. Consider the case of a hearing-impaired or completely deaf child born to hearing parents. Often the fact that the child in this situation does not (adequately) hear is not detected until the child is a toddler or older. This is the case because the child exhibits behavior that is typical of toddlers—behavior precisely like that described in the scenarios above. That is, deaf children act just like hearing children in these sorts of situations. Yet deaf children whose deafness has not yet been discovered are linguistically deprived. Only after someone recognizes that these children don't hear can linguistic information be given to them—whether in the form of access to spoken language via hearing aids, lessons in lip-reading, and/or lessons in vocaliza-

tion or in the form of teaching the child (and often the whole family) to use sign language.

In other words, long before these deaf children have access to
linguistic input, they do think, as is obvious from their thought-
demonstrating behavior. There is no possibility, however, that their
thought is in a specific human language since they have not even
begun to acquire any specific human language.

A similar kind of argument can be made by looking at the studies of Genie, a young girl who was discovered in 1970 in Los Angeles, living in captive isolation that limited both her physical
activity and linguistic input (also discussed in chapter 1). At the
time of her discovery, she could hardly walk and gave no indication of knowing what speech was. Several researchers worked for
years to teach Genie language, and although she never progressed
beyond an unsystematic stringing together of a few words, she did
manage to talk about the events of her life, including events that
had happened prior to her gaining linguistic knowledge. Clearly,
these memories constitute thought—thought that was independent
of linguistic structure.

Another way to argue that thought is not equivalent to specific language can be drawn from consideration of our vocabulary.
Have you heard the rumor that the Inuit have dozens of words for
snow? This rumor has been used as evidence in favor of the idea
that the Inuit understand differentiations in snow types that are
beyond the comprehension of, say, people from Florida, whose
vocabulary lacks the equivalent words.

The origin of this rumor doesn't matter to our discussion. What
does matter is that people have welcomed this rumor and its ensu-
ing conclusion—that the Inuit think differently from those who
do not have as rich a vocabulary for winter events. The rumor
clearly has appeal; people believe it because it seems so right to

them. The Inuit live with snow most of the year, so it makes sense that they'd have lots of words for it. Furthermore, the conclusion also has appeal. If the Inuit have words we don't have, it makes sense that they have concepts (i.e., thought) we don't have.

First, let me disabuse you of this rumor: No one, so far as I know, has ever produced evidence that Inuktitut (the language of the Inuit) does in fact, have lots of words for snow. Also, it doesn't follow that people have several words for something that occurs abundantly around them. There are many things we are surrounded by in great quantity that we do not have lots of words for. Florida beach bums, for example, do not have many words for sand. Go outside and stand in a yard and you will probably be surrounded by different kinds of weeds, yet you probably cannot name any of them, except perhaps dandelions and violets. When it comes to the range of our vocabulary, it is not abundance that matters. We are quite happy linguistically ignoring things that occur in abundance around us.

If we need to differentiate between types of something, such as snow, then we find ways to do that, regardless of our specific language and regardless of how large our vocabulary is for that something. In English we can do that for snow by using choice adjectives ("granular snow"), compounds ("powder snow"), and compound adjectives ("hard-packed snow"). American skiers can talk to each other about snow conditions in exquisite detail, whether they hail from Florida (where I never saw snow as a child) or Colorado (where the snow is a distinct presence). Likewise, a carpenter has a range of ways in which to refer to different qualities of wood—perhaps qualities that relate to the ease of carving—using the existing words in his vocabulary. Similarly, a lumberjack has many ways to refer to different qualities of wood, but her descriptions—also using ordinary vocabulary with well-chosen adjectives or compounds or compound adjectives—are more likely to be qualities that relate to the type of tree. In other words, our languages let us talk about what we want to talk about.

However, even if the rumor (that that Inuit have more words for snow) is false and its appeal is deceptive, that doesn't necessarily mean that the conclusion was false. So we must ask, if a language has a word for a given concept and another language lacks a word for that concept, does it follow that the given concept is mentally accessible to people of the first language and inaccessible to people of the second language? That is, do the two sets of speakers think differently?

In answering this question, consider your own experiences in life. When you meet a new word, are you necessarily meeting a new concept? Let's say that I ask you to mix yellow and blue paints in varying amounts and put the different colors in a set of bowls. Along the way, you happen to mix up chartreuse, but you don't know the particular word "chartreuse." If I tell you that the mix in one bowl is called chartreuse, all I've done is given you a label. But you already recognized the concept, or you wouldn't have put it in one of the bowls. That is, unless you are blind or color-blind, the actual qualities of the color precede your labeling of it. To take a more familiar example, in the United States, in voting booths many states have ballots that are punched by machine. The little parts that fall out of the ballot when it is punched are called chads. Before the presidental election of 2000, many Americans didn't know the word "chad," but they nevertheless had familiarity with the concept of one.

In these types of situations it seems rather obvious that the concept of the object can be understood without a word for that object, but what about a situation in which the concept at stake is not one of identification of a concrete object but rather of an abstract one?

Let me present two examples, contrasting English and Italian, as we consider whether the vocabulary difference between the two languages reveals a difference in thought possibilities. Italian lacks a vocabulary item corresponding to the word "privacy." Are we to conclude, then, that Italians do not understand the concept? Surely this is not a proper conclusion, and a simple observation of Italians' habits reveals this fact. Italians close the door when they use a public bathroom, they do not have sexual relations in public, and they do not ask personal questions of people they are not intimate with. In other words, they respect privacy regardless of the fact that they have no single word denoting that concept. So, although they will use a circumlocution to translate "Please respect my privacy," they understand the concept and communicate it effectively. Indeed, they have an adjective that is translated as 'private,' they simply have a lexical gap (from an English perspective) when it comes to the relevant noun.

On the other hand, Italian has the word *scaramanzia*, for which I know no single vocabulary item of English that can serve as a translation. *Scaramanzia* is the superstition that makes us say that the worst is going to happen in order to ward it off. For example, both my sisters had breast cancer, so I told my doctor (among others) that I'm bound to get it. But my fervent hope is that I won't, and there's an ignorant but nonetheless real sense in me that by saying I will get it, I've robbed that terrible evil of its power. I've been doing things like that all my life, long before I had ever heard the word *scaramanzia*. And now that I've described this to you, I'm sure you understand the concept (which doesn't mean that you share my ignorant attraction to magic), whether you've ever practiced this behavior or not. Although most Italians and Americans do not practice this behavior regularly, the fact that people of both cultures understand the concept and occasionally practice it shows that understanding the concept is independent of a vocabulary item in one's language that denotes it.

In sum, the presence and lack of the words "privacy" and *scaramanzia* in Italian and English tell us nothing whatsoever about differences between the ways English speakers and Italian speakers think.

Analogous arguments can be made by looking at vocabulary differences in any two languages. German has the word *Schadenfreude*, which is a compound of the root for "misfortune" and the root for "joy." *Schadenfreude* is the pleasure one takes in the misfortunes of others. Although you might not have experienced this pleasure, nor might many Germans, you can understand the concept, regardless of the fact that English has no such word. Often the villains in soap operas and the like are more hateful because we recognize they experience *Schadenfreude*. One language will coin a word for a given concept whereas another language will not. Scholars of various disciplines (psychology, sociology) might debate why this happens, but the important point for us is simply that the speakers of both languages can understand the concept, regardless.

You might argue that the existence of a word for a concept in a given language in some way legitimizes or licenses the concept in that linguistic community. That is, we have a word for it, so the concept must be shared by many and is, therefore, somehow more true or real than it might be without a linguistic label. This could be right. Nevertheless, the licensing of a concept is distinct from the ability to grasp that concept. In the college where I work, many first year students enter with the fear that our highly selective admissions committee made a mistake and they don't belong here. We have no single word for this fear (which is shared by first year students on many campuses, I bet) but it's easy to recognize and understand.

Vocabulary differences are not the only differences between languages, so we should turn now to other types of differences and ask what they tell us about the relationships between language and thought. Some scholars have argued that a certain population cannot reason in the same way as another population because of syntactic differences between the languages of the two populations. Instead of reporting on that literature (which would require a lengthy discussion), I'll present an analogous situation that has not been widely discussed in this light. We will look again at a contrast between Italian and English, this time focusing on sentence structure.

In English we can say, "John beat the eggs stiff," meaning that John beat the eggs with the result that they became stiff. The word "stiff" in this sentence is called a resultative secondary predicate. In Romance languages the literal translation of that sentence is not grammatical because Romance languages do not allow resultative secondary predicates in as wide a range of sentence structures as English allows. Instead, in a Romance language you'd say something that would be translated literally as "John beat the eggs until they became stiff" or "John beat the eggs to the point of (their) being stiff." A person who holds to the idea that thought is language might try to use this information to argue that Italians, Spaniards, Romanians, French, Portuguese, and speakers of other Romance languages cannot understand the concept of direct result. But that's obviously false. Speakers of Romance languages clearly understand the concept of direct result; they simply have available a different range of sentence structures to render this concept.

Analogous arguments can be built around other sentence structure differences between languages. For example, some languages express possession by a verb that can be translated as "have." But others express possession in other ways, such as by stating existence with respect to something else. For example, to express "I have a sister" in Russian one would say, *U menja sestra.* A word-by-word translation of this is "with-me-sister." (Note that there is no verb here. Typically the verb that means "be" is omitted when the present tense is to be conveyed.) Does that mean that the speakers of the first type of language (including English) have a different sense of what possession is from the speakers of the second type of language (including Russian)? In particular, do we think of sisters differently? At a certain point, the proposition that differences in structure between languages are evidence of differences in conceptual behavior between peoples leads to nonsense. In my opinion, this is one of those times.

Another argument that language and thought are not equivalent comes from the fact that we can speak without thinking. We do it much too often, are surprised at what we said, and then correct it. In fact, we can even read without thinking, coming to the end of the page and realizing that we have no idea what we've just read. And sometimes we can read aloud, thus indisputably using our language mechanism, and still think about something else, so that we lose our place in the passage and don't even know what we've read and what we haven't. This is particularly striking evidence that language and thought cannot be one and the same, nor are they even necessarily dependent on each other.

Many more arguments can be brought to bear on the question of whether thought equals language. We could ask whether animals think, and if our answer is positive (as mine is), we must abandon the notion that thought is language since animals do not have language in the sense that humans do (a point discussed in chapter 5). We could ask whether people who have brain disease or injury that robs them of language still think, and if our answer is positive, we must again abandon this notion. But even without looking at the vast amount of research on animals and on language pathologies, that is, without looking at research that goes beyond our daily experience, we can debunk certain myths about language simply by looking at the evidence available in everyday life. The myth that we think in specific languages is one of those debunkable myths, as we've seen already.

This conclusion does not minimize the importance of the various relationships that hold between language and thought. Language facilitates the introduction and transmission of thoughts, and a particular phrasing of a concept can give it a slant that offers the listener a new perspective. Sometimes we may not even be quite sure of our thoughts until we put them into language, which is one reason why talking to a confidant when making crucial decisions can be so valuable. Speaking one's mind or writing one's ideas can also help in recognizing the form of a particular rational argument we are developing. Using language can help us in analysis of many types, just as drawing what we saw can help us understand its significance. But the drawing is not tantamount to the act of seeing; likewise, expressing oneself in language is not tantamount to the act of thinking.

Language is like a hanger that we put our thoughts on. When the clothing is in a pile on the floor, it might be harder to recognize it for what it truly is. The structure of the hanger clarifies the structure of the clothing. But clarification of an essence is distinct from the essence itself.

In sum, whether or not we have words for concepts, we can and do entertain those concepts. And some concepts we may never have words for—they are ineffable.

I want to leave you with a final consideration, which again connects to daily experience—one I'd simply like to pose. Observe the following conversation between two speakers:

I hate snakes.

Do you remember Mrs. Bicknell?

Our eighth-grade social studies teacher?

Yes.

Sure I remember her. Why?

Well, when you said snakes, I remembered the day I went to
talk to her after school about how my family was falling
apart, and she asked me what the matter was and if
Patrick had walked some other girl home, and she was
so condescending that I just left and walked home
alone and saw this twisted stick by the sidewalk and I
said, "You look like a crazy snake. Hello, you crazy
snake." I thought I was alone, but Patrick was walking
right behind me and he said, "I always thought you
were crazy, but now I know."

Oh.

When the second speaker goes into that long speech, you can see
how much thought she's reporting—thought that apparently took
place between the first utterance ("I hate snakes.") and the second
("Do you remember Mrs. Bicknell?") If all that thought took place
in actual English sentences, they would have had to come at a re-
markable speed. And although the production of English in this
long thought between the first and second utterance would be free
of speech production—and thus free of the slowness of the speech
articulators (the tongue, the lips, the bottom jaw, and all the other
parts of the body that participate in speech production)—it is still
a stream of silent words, which if spoken would come as fast as a
voice recording increased to a continuous squeak. The speed of
thought exceeds that of speech, of the fastest fingers typing, and

even of a brief, meaningful look. Can silent language possibly be that fast? Ideally, we should design an experiment to measure the speed of silent language at this point. If we cannot do that, if we cannot devise some way to test whether or not silent language has the characteristics of thought (such as great speed), we are left in an unsupported position.

But even without experimental evidence, we can push the hypothesis—that language and thought are equivalent—to an absurd end by considering the language and thought of Deaf people (by "Deaf" with a capital "D", I mean people whose primary language is a sign language) with regard to speed. Signs generally take about twice as long to produce as words. So do Deaf people think twice as slowly as hearing people (since they would be thinking in visual signs)? Moreover, some Deaf people have mastered spoken languages. I have such friends, and they speak English at the ordinary rate. So do these Deaf people think at double the rate when they are speaking as when they are signing? The proposal, again, is nonsensical to me.

Thought is thought. Language is language. The two are distinct.

Further Reading

Carruthers, P., and J. Boucher, eds. 1998. *Language and thought: Interdisciplinary themes*. New York: Cambridge University Press.

Chomsky, N., and R. Anshen. 1995. *Language and thought*. Wakefield, R.I.: Moyer Bell.

Fauconnier, G. 1997. *Mappings in thought and language*. New York: Cambridge University Press.

Gumperz, J., and S. Levinson, eds. 1996. *Rethinking linguistic relativity*. New York: Cambridge University Press.

Li, P., and L. Gleitman. 2002. Turning the tables: Language and spatial reasoning. *Cognition*, 83: 265–294.

Papafragou, A., C. Massey, and L. Gleitman. 2002. Shake, rattle 'n' roll: The representation of motion in language and cognition. *Cognition*, 84: 189–219.

Pullum, G. 1991. *The great Eskimo vocabulary hoax and other irreverent essays on the study of language*. Chicago, Ill.: University of Chicago Press.

Vygotsky, L., and A. Kozulin. 1986. *Thought and language*. Cambridge, Mass.: MIT Press.

Web Sites

Gauker, C. Language and thought. http://www.uniromae.it/kant/field/lat.htm

Kaye, L. The language of thought. http://www.uniroma3.it/kant/field/lot.html

Slobin, D. Language and thought. http://www.lsadc.org/web2/lg_thought.html

The language of thought hypothesis. http://plato.stanford.edu/entries/language-thought/

4 Are sign languages real languages?

Almost all hearing people have seen Deaf people communicating with each other by moving their hands, either on television or in real life. The manual-visual language the Deaf are using is called sign language. Many hearing children know the manual alphabet used by the Deaf in America, and many hearing children and adults can make a few signs. But most hearing people do not have Deaf friends.

You might object to that last claim because you are a hearing person and you have a friend who has been losing or has already lost his hearing as he grew older. So I want to make a distinction here between people whose first language is a spoken language and who lose their hearing through injury, disease, or aging, and most important, who never use a sign language as their major means of communication—who are typically called deaf people (with a small "d")—and people who are hard of hearing or cannot hear at all (for whatever reason) and who use a sign language as their major means of communication—who are called Deaf people (with a capital "D"). People in the first group are integrated into hearing society; people in the second group are generally not.

Again, you might object to that last claim, but let me give you a point of comparison. There are about 24 million deaf or hard-of-hearing people in the United States, of which a significant percentage are Deaf—estimates range up to around 3 million, although it may be more like 2 million (see the Gallaudet Research Institute figures on demographics at http://www.gri.gaulladet.edu). Compare these figures to those for Jewish Americans: There are at most around 6 million Jewish people in the United States, fewer than half of whom claim synagogue membership (see the Jerusalem Center for Public Affairs figures on demographics at http://www.jcpa.org). So there might be about the same number of Deaf people as there are synagogue members in the United States. Yet many people who are not members of synagogues have Jewish friends who are members of synagogues. In contrast, very few hearing people have Deaf friends. Simply put, Deaf people in America are part of a separate culture.

Why? The answer to this question is going to be long and involves answering the main question of this chapter—that is, whether or not sign languages are real languages. Furthermore, since access to language is not just a basic human right but also the means by which so many of our civil rights are delivered, the fact that many deaf and hard-of-hearing people have experienced at least partial blockage to language access (particularly access to the majority language of a culture) means that they have experienced a curtailment of rights. For this reason, this chapter also dips into the relationship between language and civil rights.

I'd like you to gather nine friends (plus you, to make a total of ten) who do not sign and play a game that is similar to charades. Give each friend a numbered index card with a sentence on it, such as the following:

1. I'm scared.
2. You're tall.
3. He's mean.
4. Let's swim.
5. I'm hungry.
6. That lion is happy.

7. Where's the dog?
8. How did you do that?
9. Why do you think Marilyn Monroe got mixed up with JFK?
10. What did your aunt say last Tuesday when you confessed you lost her entire life savings at the racetrack?

Now, going in order of the numbers on the cards, each person should do whatever is necessary to make the others guess the sentence on the card without saying or mouthing any words. (If you hate the idea of using friends, try doing it yourself, in front of a mirror.) It is likely that the game will be easy at first and get increasingly difficult as you go through the numbered sentences. Notice how simple sentences 7 and 8 are yet how difficult it is to communicate them without language. Sentences 9 and 10 should have left you at a loss.

Have a discussion with your friends about why some sentences were easier to guess than others. Pointing makes talking about "I" or "you" or "he" quite easy. But you can't use pointing alone to talk about "that lion" or "the dog" or "Marilyn Monroe" or "JFK" or "your aunt." Ideas in the words "scared," "mean," "happy," "tall," and "swim" are relatively easy to transmit by facial expressions, by raising your hand, or by mimicking swimming motions. But it's more difficult to use such simple methods to indicate the ideas in the words "where," "how," "why," "mixed up," "confessed," "think," "say," and so on. And how do you act out time frames, especially points in time as particular as "last Tuesday"?

The information in all of those English sentences can easily be conveyed in sign language. In fact, any sentence in English or any other spoken language could be conveyed in sign language. Sign languages can communicate information about people and objects that are not present (so they can't be pointed to), about specific times (in the past, in the future, and now), and about very particular events (such as forgetting to buy the candles the kindergarten teacher asked you to pick up). Think about what this means concerning the relationship between the structural form of an individual sign and its meaning. For most signs, that relationship must not be predictable; in fact, it must be arbitrary.

The last sentence might strike you as strange, but think about spoken language. Why do English speakers call a chicken a chicken? Why do we call shoes shoes? There is nothing about the sound of the word "chicken" or the sound of the word "shoes" that makes us able to guess their meaning. If languages worked in such a way, we might be able to guess the meaning of most words in most languages, but we can't. Can you guess the meaning of the Chinese word jiε ("chicken")? Can you guess the meaning of the Italian word *scarpe* ("shoes")? In any given word in any spoken language, the correspondence between sound and meaning is typically abitrary because for most words no other possibility arises.

The kinds of words that would be open to a nonarbitrary correspondence between meaning and sound are words whose meaning has to do with sound. When we say that a bee "buzzes," we might think that the meaning of the word "buzz" sounds like the actual word, and so we might feel that there's a predictable correspondence between meaning and sound. Such words are called onomatopoetic. Actually, though, if you look at the English words whose meanings are sounds (especially words that mean the noises animals make, like "meow" or "moo" or "cockadoodledoo"), you will find that their counterparts in other languages are often (probably usually) not recognizable. In fact, when speakers of one language are asked to guess at the meaning of so-called onomatopoetic words in other languages, their guesses vary widely. Thus the whole idea of onomatopoeia is questionable.

But even if you believe that some words are onomatopoetic, it's clear that most words are not and could not be because the meaning of most words is not concerned with particular sounds. In studies in which linguists have asked people why a given word means what it does, the people can't answer. The very question is a puzzle because language is not organized to have a predictable correspondence between sound and meaning, and we know this fact even if we've never explicitly discussed it. In one study, a bowl of spaghetti was put in front of a Canadian speaker of English. He was asked why he called it spaghetti. He looked at the linguist, baffled. Then he said something to this effect: "It looks like spaghetti. It smells like spaghetti." He took a bite. "It is spaghetti."

Therefore, we can feel more comfortable with the fact that the relationship between the structure of a sign and its meaning is for the most part arbitrary. Sign languages are like spoken languages in that their vocabulary is characterized as having an arbitrary relationship between form (whether a manual structure or sounds) and meaning.

Although this fact is utterly natural, given everything you know about language, many people have trouble believing it. It is not uncommon to find assumptions or even outright claims to the contrary—essentially, claims that signs are iconic. Iconicity is as impossible for most signs as onomatopoeia is for most words. To see that, we need to know what the structure of a sign is.

Hold out your dominant hand (the one you write with). Since most of us are right-handed, I will assume that you have your right hand out now—so, if you are left-handed, make the necessary changes in what follows. Straighten all your fingers and your palm, and keep all the fingers close beside one another, excepting the thumb. Now hold this flat hand in front of your ribs, with the palm facing down and the fingertips facing away from the body. Move your wrist from the center of your body to the side of your body (if your right hand is extended, you are moving it from left to right), so that your flat hand hits a starting point and then lightly bounces in the air to an ending point. (It's as though you pat one place in the air, then raise your hand over, simply by a movement of the wrist, and pat a second place in the air.) If my directions are good enough, you've made the American Sign Language (ASL) sign CHILDREN (signs are always written in capitals, by convention).

(If you have access to the web, you might want to go to an ASL dictionary and view the sign. I recommend the site http://commtechlab.msu.edu/sites/aslweb/. But if you cannot access the web now, I will continue describing signs.)

Now do the same movement (bouncing from left to right) of that same flat hand, but this time with the palm facing up. You've made the ASL sign SOMETHING. Thus the orientation of the palm matters in distinguishing one sign from another.

Now hold both hands in front of you, palms touching each other, with the right (the dominant) palm facing down and the other facing up. Keep the palms touching as you hold the left hand stationary and move the right hand with that same flick of the wrist from left to right. (You can't bounce the top hand here since it stays in contact with the bottom hand.) You've made the ASL sign CHEESE. (Actually, in isolation this sign typically involves repetition of the wrist motion. But in quick conversation, just one flick of the wrist can do.) Therefore, the location of where you move the dominant hand (in front of your ribs or in the location of on top of your other hand) matters. In other words the place a sign is made matters in distinguishing one sign from another.

Now move your dominant hand back to the place in front of your ribs and face this flat hand palm downward again. Move the wrist—but this time move it so that the tips of the fingers go up and down. You've made the ASL sign BOUNCE. Movement matters in distinguishing one sign from another.

Now keep your dominant hand in front of your ribs, palm downward, and do the old movement of the wrist from side to side, with the bounce you had as you did CHILDREN. But this time stick out straight only your thumb, index finger, and middle finger, all three spread, and let your two last fingers curl under. You've made the ASL sign THIRTY-THREE. Thus the handshape matters in distinguishing one sign from another.

From looking at just five different signs, we can see that four parameters are important in talking about the structure of a sign: palm orientation, location, movement, and hand shape. There are other parameters of signs, but consideration of just these four is adequate for our following discussion.

We are still investigating the issue of iconicity in sign languages. If a sign were to be iconic, there would have to be a non-arbitrary relationship between its structure and its meaning. Because we typically view structure in a sign language (as we hear structure in a spoken language), the sign would have to look like what it meant. That is, somehow the combination of parameters that make up a sign would have to look like the meaning of the sign. What kinds of signs, then, even have the potential to be iconic? These are signs whose meanings have to do with physical objects whose shape the hand(s) can reasonably assume and/or with a stance or movement that the hands can reasonably mimic.

Hold out your dominant hand again. Extend the index and middle fingers straight and spread, and curl the other three under so that the thumb tip closes over the other two fingertips. If you held this hand shape in front of you with the palm facing out and the extended fingertips facing up, you would have the V sign for victory in ordinary gestures. Now give the nondominant hand the same flat hand shape we used in the first five signs. Point the extended fingertips of the dominant hand downward so that they rest on the palm of the nondominant hand. You have made the sign STAND. See how the two extended fingers look like a person's legs standing on the nondominant palm? If you now bend the extended fingers, so they lose contact with the nondominant palm, and then extend them, making contact again, you've made the sign JUMP. And if you bend them and make contact with the nondominant palm while the extended fingers are bent, so that the knuckles are on the palm, you've made the sign KNEEL.

These sorts of signs seem about as close to iconic as signs can get. But let's do the same kinds of tests that I talked about for onomatopoeia. Make the sign KNEEL and ask people who don't know any ASL what it means. When I do that with classes, their responses very a great deal. But if I show them the sign STAND and tell them what it means and then I show them the sign KNEEL, they can usually guess correctly. So it's really only once the analogy is pointed out to them (between the two active fingers and the legs of a person) that they can use whatever degree of iconicity there are in these signs to figure out the meaning. Furthermore, if you look at the counterparts to these signs in other sign languages around the world, it won't be easier to guess what they mean than it is to guess the meaning of so-called onomatopoetic words in spoken languages. In other words, if iconicity exists at all in sign languages, it affects only a tiny part of the vocabulary.

You can convince yourself of the fact that the vocabulary of sign languages has an arbitrary correspondence between structure and meaning just by looking at any two Deaf people who are signing together. If signs were truly iconic, we'd be able to guess the meaning of a conversation without knowing the sign language at all. But we can't.

I discussed the four parameters of a sign because only by appreciating a hint of the complexity of the structure of signs can most people truly believe that sign languages are bona fide languages. It is important to understand that fact if we, as a society, are to make responsible decisions about language policy and the Deaf—decisions I address later in this chapter.

For now I want to make one final point about signing, which I hope will not confound the previous conclusion. Although individual signs are not iconic, often in signing a conversation a certain amount of drawing in the air takes place. Let's say that someone wants to sign the sense of the sentence "I was driving along and I saw flames shooting out of a tall apartment building on my left, so I stopped and ran across the street into a pharmacy to get help." As part of signing this, she will probably indicate a building that is an apartment on the left side of the signing space in front of her and point to the top of that building before she makes the sign for flames. She will also probably move her finger from that apartment building to the right side of the signing space in front of her to indicate that the pharmacy is directly across the street from the apartment building. She might use the sign RUN, or she might move her finger quickly to the position in the signing space that she has set up for the pharmacy. These parts of signing the sentence—indicating relative position and the type of movement by going slowly or quickly—are similar to drawing in the air. It's no surprise that sign language does this because sign is received visually.

All the discussion up to this point has helped us to understand that sign languages are real languages—they are not merely unstructured gestures, nor are they iconic. So learning to sign and to understand sign in any sign language is a task similar to learning to speak and to understand in any spoken language. This means that a hearing person will have to study ASL if she wants to communicate with Deaf people in ASL. But what does that mean for a Deaf person who wants to communicate with hearing people in English? In the

United States, English is the lingua franca, which people who use a minority language must usually learn, not vice versa.

This chapter, then, really needs to continue, facing two additional important questions: Can a Deaf person learn to speak English? Can a Deaf person learn to understand spoken English?

Many Deaf people have spent years and years in learning to speak English with little or no success. Some, on the other hand, have learned to speak so well that hearing strangers can often understand them. Deaf people in this latter group are a tiny minority (I'll discuss why in the section on oral education below.) Many Deaf people have tried for years to read lips, with moderate or little success, although some have great success. Again, the latter are in the minority. (And, again, I'll discuss why below.)

The job of a Deaf person who is learning to speak a language and read lips is dauntingly more difficult than that of a hearing person who is learning to sign and understand sign. Most Deaf people do not succeed—and the educational and emotional cost for those who do succeed can be very high.

We're finally ready to return to the question of why Deaf people have a separate culture from hearing people. If you are Deaf in America and do not speak English, and you meet a person who is hearing who does not sign in ASL, it is extremely hard for the two of you to understand each other beyond the most rudimentary level. Therefore, a meaningful friendship is all but precluded. Business interactions are possible if they proceed through written language, but actually working together is not possible if it calls for significant nonwritten language interaction. All of these facts lead to the likelihood of hearing people and Deaf people going their separate ways, and hence having separate cultures.

That Deaf and hearing people should have separate cultures is not a problem per se. No matter who you are, you probably belong to several different subcultures, defined by your race, ethnicity, religion, and hobbies (like bowling or card playing or even something like beer drinking), among others. The problem is that Deaf people are precluded from the huge majority culture that absorbs all the hearing people. Because of this preclusion, the rights of Deaf people have not been fairly protected.

Before I go into the question of rights, however, I want to point out that Deaf people do not have to be excluded from hearing culture. There is a very well-known and studied case of a community on Martha's Vineyard, Massachusetts, with a large population of congenitally Deaf people. The hearing population on the island decided to accommodate this minority population by learning ASL. In a store, for example, if a group of hearing people were having a conversation and a Deaf couple arrived, the language would change to ASL and the Deaf couple could participate fully in the conversation. Social life and business life, essentially all culture on the island, were open to anyone, hearing or Deaf. The last Deaf person in that original population died in the 1950s, and ASL has since disappeared from the island. But for quite a while we had what I consider the ideal situation for a society that wants to welcome Deaf people into the majority culture.

Society should want to ensure the civil rights of all its members, and undoubtedly the best way to ensure the civil rights of the Deaf is to allow them access to the majority culture. The Deaf have to become literate in the majority language to participate economically and educationally in the majority culture. But if the hearing were also to become minimally fluent in sign, the Deaf could participate in the whole range of civil rights that the majority culture enjoys, as well as in its social interactions. In other words, with some flexing of linguistic muscles by both hearing and nonhearing populations, the society could protect a segment of its population that has suffered from a lack of such protection: Language is the key.

We are now ready to discuss two important issues regarding language policy and the Deaf. One involves the right to be informed and to inform. The other involves the right to an education.

When the medical community around the world became aware of the contagious nature of AIDS, a vast public information campaign took place in many countries. In the United States, leaflets were printed in many languages and distributed widely in communities where English was not the dominant language. But no effort was made to inform Deaf communities, despite the fact that most Deaf people in the United States have some difficulty in reading English. (I will return to this fact below.) As a result, AIDS spread among the Deaf in a degree far worse than among hearing communities. Who knows how long this might have gone on if it hadn't been for the activism of Harry Woosley, Jr., who started the Deaf AIDS Project in 1990 (http://www.hivdent.org)? Not informing the Deaf has had catastrophic results on Deaf populations around the world.

Why did our government and our medical community ignore the rights of the Deaf? One reason is quite simple: In general the Deaf have been invisible. When figures about literacy rates among various groups in the United States are published, Latinos are often at the bottom of the list. But, in fact, Native Americans fare worse, and the Deaf fare a great deal worse. Because hearing people typically do not communicate with Deaf people, it's easy, and criminal, for the hearing to forget about the Deaf entirely.

It is partially due to the work of linguists that the rights of Deaf people are starting to be protected. In 1960 William Stokoe's book *Sign Language Structure* made it obvious that ASL is a natural human language. Linguists have since produced articles, books, and journals that analyze ASL and other sign languages around the world. Many colleges and universities all over the United States now accept ASL as fulfilling the undergraduate language requirement. In fact, over thirty states accept ASL as fulfilling the high school language requirement. Once sign languages are recognized as bona fide languages, it is impossible not to recognize that being Deaf does not entail a mental handicap. Until recent times there have been popular misconceptions to that effect, and it is our unfortunate history to have often overlooked the rights of the mentally handicapped. So this, too, is another reason behind the failure to protect the rights of Deaf people.

Under the 1990 Americans with Disabilities Act, Deaf people now have the right to an interpreter in many situations, including all legal procedings and all medical procedures, paid for by the courts and the medical profession.

The second right I want to talk about involves education. I have found very little information about the education of the deaf in the Western world before 1750. Some references cite attempts to make them hear—blowing trumpets in their ears; ringing loud bells; and pouring oil, milk, garlic juice, or eel fat into their ears. None of the results was positive, as you might well imagine. The idea that the deaf were mentally deficient was prevalent, and they did not enjoy ordinary civil rights. But in the 1500s several glimmers of enlightenment appeared. A physician in Italy spoke out against the view that the deaf were idiots. In 1575 a lawyer in Spain named Lasso defended the right of the deaf to bear children. Also, some education of the deaf began.

In the early 1500s a Spanish priest tutored a boy who had become deaf at the age of three. The boy became a famous artist, El Mudo ("the mute") and studied with Tiziano of Italy. He was eventually the court artist for King Philip II of Spain. In 1550 a monk from Spain, Pablo Ponce de Leon, set up a school for deaf children in a monastery in San Salvador. When he died, Juan Pablo Bonet and Manuel Ramirez de Carrion continued his work. In 1620 Bonet published a text on how to teach the deaf. This school developed the manual alphabet that is the basis for our finger spelling today.

Despite these efforts, before 1750, there was no hope of literacy or education for almost every deaf person in the Western world. But in 1755 Abbé de l'Epée, a cleric who was appalled by the bestial living conditions of the deaf in Paris, set up the National Institution for Deaf-Mutes. He used a combination of the signs and finger spelling of local Deaf communities to teach them. One of the teachers at the school, Abbé Roch-Ambroise Sicard, was particularly effective. Sicard trained his Deaf pupil Massieu to be a teacher at the school, and Massieu in turn trained another deaf pupil, Laurent Clerc, to be a teacher. In 1816 Clerc joined Thomas Gallaudet, a hearing man with a Deaf wife, and went to the United States to set up the American Asylum for the Deaf in Hartford, Connecticut. They brought with them French Sign Language (LSF), but their pupils, of course, used a local sign language.

Let me make an aside. What do you think of the common idea that Deaf people all around the world use the same sign language? It's wrong. Even if it were the case—which it probably is not—that all language originated with a single population of people, language changes over time. As various subpopulations migrate to different places, their language will change in different ways, yielding new languages. Also, the language of the population that is left behind will change, yielding a new language. Over time the languages become more and more distinct from one another, until they are mutually incomprehensible. This is the way of language, and always has been. Thus the Deaf in Beijing, Tokyo, Johannesburg,

Berlin, Moscow, Sydney, Jakarta, and everywhere else use sign languages that are all different.

What's going to happen when you throw together two populations of Deaf people, using mutually incomprehensible sign languages, and tell them they have to work together? The stage is set for a pidgin—a kind of slapdash contact language that will allow rudimentary communication—which is what happened at the Hartford school. But pidgins don't last. The generation of Deaf who were exposed only to this pidgin (not to LSF nor to the local Hartford sign language) came up with a creole, which is exactly what occurs with spoken language. A creole has all the expressive capacity of any natural language, as well as all the structure (although, as is discussed in chapter 8, particular characteristics of structure tend to be common among creoles no matter what languages they evolved from).

ASL was the result of LSF meeting local Hartford sign language, which is, by its history, a creole. It has many things in common with LSF and with other sign languages genetically related to LSF. (Italian Sign Language, for example, is another creole that developed when LSF came in contact with local Italian sign languages.) But, importantly, it has no special relationship to English because the language of the hearing historically had almost no impact on the language of the Deaf. So, for example, British Sign Language, which is not genetically related to LSF, is extremely different from ASL—the two are mutually incomprehensible.

The success of the school in Hartford (which later changed its name to the American School for the Deaf) led Congress in 1864 to pass a law that authorized the Columbia Institution for the Deaf and Blind in Washington, D.C. This was the first institution of higher learning specifically for the Deaf and blind.

Did it make sense to put the Deaf and blind together? Are their special educational needs similar? The blind do not form a language community, and they speak exactly like the seeing. Misconceptions about these handicaps were responsible for putting the Deaf and blind together. Nevertheless, the establishment of this institution must be applauded as a milestone. Its first principal was Edward Gallaudet, the son of Thomas, and it was later rechristened Gallaudet University. It is one of the most important educational institutions for the Deaf in the world.

By 1867 there were twenty-six schools for the Deaf around the United States. Today there are several institutions of higher learning for the Deaf, many of them technical colleges, like the National Technical Institute for the Deaf in Rochester, New York. There are also some famous grade schools for the Deaf, such as the Lexington School for the Deaf in New York City, which educates children from 0 to 21 years old.

All was going very well. But in the 1870s a debate began, for which Alexander Graham Bell was largely responsible, that resulted in a huge setback for the education of Deaf people in the United States. Bell and others argued that by educating the Deaf in sign language, they were isolated from the hearing community. Therefore the Deaf should not be allowed to sign but instead should be taught to vocalize and to lip-read.

So-called oral schools sprang up. In 1880 an international Congress of Educators of the Deaf in Milan, Italy, condemned the use of sign in deaf classrooms. Overnight, signing was prohibited in most classrooms in the Western world. By 1907 there were 197 schools for the deaf in the United States, and none of them used ASL. Let's think about what it would be like to try to vocalize if you couldn't hear. Listen to a newborn, whose vocal tract makes lots of noises that don't sound like human language, as well as lots of noises that do sound very much like human language. From about seven months on in the womb, fetuses are listening to the world inside and outside their mother. They have a lot of experience with human language by the time they are born, yet they still produce many nonlanguage sounds. What if the babies had had no previous human language experience? Maybe the sounds they would produce at birth would be even less like human language. How would we teach them to produce human language sounds if they couldn't hear them?

Let's say that someone plugs the ears of a hearing person and then brings him to Thailand and asks him to learn to speak Thai. No aural input of Thai is available. How does he do it? If he already knows another spoken language, he has a headstart, of course, because spoken languages have in common major distinctions between sounds, such as consonant sounds versus vowel sounds. He also knows that the teeth, tongue, vocal cords, lungs, nasal cavity, and lips are all involved in making language sounds. But how can he learn exactly where to place his tongue in his mouth when making a sound if he cannot compare his mimicking of that sound? How can he learn exactly the right amount of tightening of his vocal cords or exactly the right amount of pressing of his lips or any number of other factors relevant to producing the quality of particular sounds without the benefit of checking his mimic against a model?

Oral schools used many methods, including rewards when the production of a word got close to the model and punishments when it didn't. Teachers put students' hands on the teachers' throats, cheeks, or lips to help them feel the external effects of what was happening inside the speech tract. The information you can gain in this way is highly limited.

What about trying to read lips? Mouth the words "pat," "bat," and "mat" to a friend across the room. Your friend almost assuredly will not be able to distinguish among them because the differences occur inside the vocal tract at places you cannot see. With the initial sound in "pat," the vocal cords are not vibrating rapidly, but with the initial sounds in "bat" and "mat" they are. With the initial sound in "mat," the air flows continuously out through the nose, but with the initial sounds in "pat" and "bat" it does not. The longer the word is, the more opportunities there are for multiple readings of sounds if the only information you have is looking at the face of the person speaking. I have read that even the very best lip-reader gets only about 60% of the material, and most lipreaders do not approach that figure. Imagine the miscommunications and frustrations that occur with such an error rate.

In oral schools, children spent years just trying to learn to vocalize and lip-read. Often they were taught very little mathematics, geography, history, or literature in an effort to teach them vocalization and lip-reading. In other words, these schools were trying hard to essentially undo deafness, rather than to educate the Deaf.

It's no surprise that oralism failed miserably. In the 1850s, in the heyday of Deaf education in ASL, the graduates of the Hartford asylum were as literate as the hearing population. But by 1972, the average reading level of the eighteen-year-old Deaf high school graduate in the United States was at a fourth-grade level. A similar situation prevailed in Britain.

Today, most Deaf children in the United States either are in special schools for the Deaf, which are bilingual-bicultural ASL-English, or are mainstreamed into hearing schools but with extra support classes and aides who interpret for them. Nevertheless, oral schools persist in some communities. As figures on literacy become available, however, these schools tend to convert to the bilingual-bicultural model. We are on the way to restoring to Deaf people the right to education, a right that we as a society took away because of the misconception that the Deaf would be better off if their deafness was ignored. When it comes to language, however, deafness cannot and should not be ignored.

All of this discussion has brought us back full circle to my opening claim that most hearing people do not have Deaf friends. By and large, it is the lack of exposure of the hearing to the Deaf that is responsible for the misconception that sign languages are not real languages and for many of the social injustices that the Deaf have experienced. If you are motivated now to learn ASL, look in the phone book under local public services. There is a deaf and hearing interaction center in almost every urban area, and in many rural areas as well.

Further Readings

Bornstein, H., ed. 1990. *From manual communication: Implications for education.* Washington, D.C.: Gallaudet University Press.

Cohen, H. 1994. *Train go sorry: Inside a Deaf world.* Boston, Mass.: Houghton Mifflin.

Klima, E., U. Bellugi, and R. Battison. 1979. *The signs of language.* Cambridge, Mass.: Harvard University Press.

Kyle, J., and B. Woll, eds. 1983. *Language in sign.* London: Croom Helm.

————. 1985. *Sign language: The study of Deaf people and their language.* Cambridge: Cambridge University Press.

Messing, C. 1999. *Gestures, speech, and sign.* New York: Oxford University Press.

Neidle, C., J. Kegl, D. MacLaughlin, B. Bahan, and R. Lee. 1999. *The syntax of American Sign Language: Functioning categories and hierarchical structure.* Cambridge, Mass.: MIT Press.

Sacks, O. 1989. *Seeing voices.* Berkeley: University of California Press.

Stokoe, W. 1960. *Sign language structure: An outline of visual communication systems of the American Deaf.* Silver Spring, Md.: Linstok Press.

———. 1965. *A dictionary of American Sign Language on Linguistic Principles*. Silver Spring, Md.: Linstok Press.
Wilbur, R. 1979. *American Sign Language and sign systems*. Baltimore, Md.: University Park Press.

Further Web Site Readings

American Sign Language Browser. http://commtechlab.msu.edu/sites/aslweb/browser.htm
Japanese Sign Language. http://tgssvr.tgs.co.jp/signlist.htm
British Sign Language. http//:www.britishsignlanguage.com/
Family Service Foundation's Deaf AIDS project. http://www.deafvision.net/dap/people/htm
Hivdent (about HIV). http://www.hivdent.org

5 Do animals have language?

You may have heard of Koko, the gorilla, or you may have read about bee dances. Many people, including some biologists, think that these examples show that animals have language. One of the biggest issues in this question is determining exactly what language is. I began an informal investigation, surveying a variety of people on the definition of "language." The first person I asked kept returning to the notion of the passing of information. Undoubtedly some instances of language involve the passing of information. But let's say I find that a branch has fallen off the big, old silver maple in my front yard, exposing a core of rot. I now know that my tree is sick. Information has been received, but did an event of language occur? Surely not, as my tree does not use language. So the passing of information cannot be sufficient grounds for calling an event an instance of language.

Someone else talked about communication, but with a different slant. She talked about a sense of purpose—about communication in which the source intends to send a message. Again, there's no doubt that language can be a type of purposeful communication. But let's say I'm sick of the mess in my son's bedroom, so I sweep it all together into a giant pile that blocks the entrance to his room. When he comes home, he puts everything away where it should go. I sent a message; he received it. Communication occurred, and on purpose. But sweeping his junk into a pile is not an instance of language. We have myriad ways to communicate, many of which do not involve language, and this is one of them.

What, then, do you know about language? You might respond that it involves sounds, and spoken language certainly does. But we write to each other, and we sign to each other as well. So not all language instances involve sounds. Furthermore, we can make many sounds that aren't part of language. Sound is neither necessary nor sufficient for an event of language to occur.

You know a lot about language.

Why, for instance, is:

the into runs sweetlying never clouds

not an utterance you might expect to hear? And how is it different from other unusual utterances, like this famous one by Noam Chomsky:

Colorless green ideas sleep furiously.

Both utterances are nonsense, but the first one is really much worse. It's wrong in more ways than the second one, which seems to be a well-formed sentence structurally, although it simply makes no sense. The first one isn't even anything we'd call a sentence.

The description of a language, what linguists call a grammar, involves the explicit statement of many rules. There are various types of rules—rules about sound and word formation, as well as sentence structure and meaning—and we apply them without conscious knowledge that we are doing so. But we easily recognize when the rules are violated. The first nonsense utterance above is terrible because a variety of rules for word structure, sentence structure, and meaning are violated—whether or not you can state precisely which rules are involved. I could have made the same point by using analogous examples from any human language in the world, including any sign language (but I would have had to provide a video of someone demonstrating nonsense signs). A grammar, then, is a collection of rules that describes a language, and a grammar is a definitional part of what makes something a language.

What else do you know about language? In the first nonsense utterance, there is something wrong with the position of "the." A preposition follows it, and in English "the" shouldn't be followed by a preposition. Also, the word "clouds" is too far away from "the." Whatever specific thing you noticed, you know that the position of "the" is somehow wrong. Did anyone ever teach you the rules for the position of "the" in an English sentence? If you are a native speaker of English, you simply knew. You learned it on your own without anyone explicitly teaching you. This is another one of the important facts about language: We have the ability to acquire language without any formal instruction in it. We are set up, hardwired, to learn it. This is another definitional part of language—its innateness (see chapter 1 for more information).

Consider the range of things that you can say, such as a sentence like this:

Hey, kids, your mother left last night, but, don't worry, she'll be back when she's come to terms with the whole notion of mortality.

(This was said tongue in cheek by a friend, but it's a useful example.) By uttering certain sounds in a given order, the speaker of this sentence is addressing particular individuals (the kids), referring to a particular individual who isn't there (their mother), referring to times that are not the present (last night and whenever the mother comes to terms), and referring to abstract ideas (worry and mortality). Let me point out in particular that the ability to refer to things that are not physically present (objects here, and times) is known as displacement. Both displacement and the ability to refer to abstractions are common to all human languages.

Now consider this sentence:

> To make a really good pasta with pesto, you need to buy a flat, long pasta that is just a little wider than linguine— called trenette—and when the pasta is almost finished being boiled, you have to add string beans (thin ones—or else cut them lengthwise in half) and very thinly sliced potatoes to the pot.

The person hearing this utterance might well choose to go shopping for trenette, string beans, and potatoes, but we would not expect him to head for the hardware store or go outside and dig a fish pond. Under normal conditions, humans process the information that comes to them through language, and they show it by reacting in ways that are typically neither random nor simply reflexes. Language involves cognitive processing.

Finally, notice that there are plenty of sentences in this chapter that you've never read or heard before. Human language is creative; it allows us to express novel ideas rather than simply to repeat a closed set of utterances.

There are more things we could say about language, but these six are enough to help us judge whether the instances of animal behavior described below are evidence of language of the type found among humans. So we'll be looking for evidence of

1. rules that might constitute a grammar
2. innateness
3. displacement

4. the ability to refer to abstractions
5. cognitive processing
6. the ability to create novel language expressions

Research on animal language has included the study of bees, birds, sea mammals, and various primates some of these studies deal with pheromones, scents involved primarily in sexual behavior. Here I'm going to look at other types of phenomena that potentially offer better candidates for language status. Observations of bees have shown that honeybee communities send out scouts to look for food. When food is located, the scouts return to the hive and recruit other bees to help them bring back the food. First, the recruiter gives the others a sample of the food, so they'll know their goal. Next, the recruiter performs a dance that identifies the location of the food. The dance can have two shapes: The "round" dance is circular and is used when the food is within 100 meters of the hive; the "wagging" dance involves a stretched-out figure eight and is used when the food is farther away. The rate at which the bee does the wagging dance conveys the distance to the food source; the farther it is, the slower the bee dances. Also, the vigor of the waggle indicates the quality of the food.

Distance is not the only information needed; the bees also have to know the direction to the food source. With the round dance, there seems to be no indication of direction, perhaps because the short distance makes it less important to have this information. With the wagging dance, however, direction is indicated by the orientation of the bee's head. The hive is typically vertical. If the top of the hive is taken to be coincidental with the location of the sun and if the bee faces straight ahead when performing the dance, the food source lies directly below the sun. If the bee's head is angled sixty degrees off the vertical, for example, then the food is located at a sixty-degree angle from the sun.

The dances of four species of honeybees have been studied so far, and in three of those species the dancing bee produced a low-frequency sound that seems to be essential in conveying the information. These three species perform their dance in the light or in the dark; that is, they do not have to have optimal visual circumstances. The one species that is silent during the dance always performs in daylight. Thus sound might well be adding information in cases in which the bees might miss visual information.

The bees who witness the dance generally arrive at the food source without much difficulty, but sometimes there are problems. If there is a barrier between the hive and the food source, the recruiter bee cannot give directions around it. Instead, the other bees fly in a straight path toward the food source; when they meet the barrier, they typically fly up and over it even if the path the recruiter bee flew in returning to the hive was shorter. Eventually, they learn shortcuts on their own. Also, if the hive has fallen or been knocked askew so that the combs are not vertical, the recruiter bee will orient the dance as though the representation of the sun is the actual direction of the sun, rather than the top of the hive. But if the hive is in a dark enclosure, as when scientists put it in a box for experimental purposes, the dance is ineffective in conveying information about the location of the food source.

Although this description is brief and incomplete, the general gist should be apparent. Given this, is the bee dance a form of language? It certainly has rules (as in 1), exhibits displacement in referring to food sources that aren't present (as in 3), and gives evidence of cognitive processing (as in 5). If the quality of the food source can be considered an abstraction, then these dances have the ability to refer to abstractions (as in 4). I haven't read about any scientific tests for innateness of these dances, although some researchers simply assume it, but creativity seems lacking. That is, although bees can indicate a range of location and quality, the parameters on what they can express are extremely limited. They cannot stray even slightly from these parameters. For example, they cannot convey that a new food source is near another well-known food source. Certainly communication takes place among bees, but are these three (or four) features of human language enough for us to call bee dances an instance of language as we understand that notion for humans?

Birdsong has also been extensively studied, and it is undisputed that birdsong transmits information. Such messages as

Here I am/ Let's mate/ There's a predator nearby/ I found food/ I found water/ The nest is over here

have been observed and documented. Songs differ from species to species, and even within species songs can vary somewhat by the territory the bird occupies. That is, bird species can have song dialects. New Zealand saddleback males, when mating with a female from another territory (typically a widow), can adopt her dialect quickly (sometimes within ten minutes) and move into the new territory. So birds can learn dialects, and in fact they can learn a second song (analogous to a second language). They can even become polycantors (analogous to polyglots, those who speak many languages), mimicking the song of other species and sometimes even nonbird sounds (e.g., noises of chainsaws or car alarms). It also appears that newly hatched birds immediately begin to acquire song, so they must be hard-wired for this task. Experiments with hand-raised white-crown sparrows show that young males who do not hear adult males' songs within the first several months of life never develop a typical courtship-territorial song. Thus it seems that birds have a critical period for acquiring song, just as humans have a critical period for acquiring language (see chapter 1).

The structure of songs also observes rules. For example, robins' song has several motifs that can be repeated in varying degrees, but these motifs must occur in a certain order or other birds will find the song unintelligible. At the same time, however, a fair amount of improvisation is observed, allowing the bird to express, perhaps, things like mood. In fact, when hens and turkeys and many other kinds of birds confront each other for the first time, they generally stop and face each other and make a variety of noises. Then they might attack, go in different directions, or feed side by side. Given this range of reactions, it seems that the birds are able to convey a range of information and that the responses are not preprogrammed but, instead, the product of cognitive processing.

To what extent then, is birdsong similar to human language? It appears to follow rules, to be innate, and to involve cognitive processing. It doesn't seem to have displacement, as birds don't have songs about predators that passed by yesterday; they are able to refer only to those that are present. Songs can refer to abstractions in a limited way (danger or happiness). As with bees, it's clear that birdsong can convey many things. The parameters of that information are not so obvious with birds as they are with bees. Still, it does not appear that birds can tell each other about what just happened to them on the other side of the barn, for example.

One might argue that birdsong is language of the type used by humans based purely on the claim that birds can learn human language—so they must have the capacity for language. Such a claim might be made after reading about Alex, an African grey parrot that Dr. Irene Pepperberg of the University of Arizona has worked with. Alex has an extensive vocabulary, supposedly comparable to that of a four- or five-year-old child. He can identify objects verbally, with

English words, by their material, color, shape, and number. He can distinguish between objects according to any of these criteria. He knows the names of certain foods, such as "nut," and he asks for them even when they are not present, exhibiting displacement. He uses words that express emotions correctly and even apologizes when he misbehaves, exhibiting the ability to refer to abstractions. So does he have language? He has certainly learned to manipulate vocal tokens to give and get desired responses, and this facility would be explained if birds had a brain mechanism similar to the human language mechanism. Nevertheless, Dr. Pepperberg warns that Alex does not talk as humans talk. His verbal behavior is erratic, and she does not claim that he has language.

The sea mammals most studied with regard to language are whales and dolphins. During mating season, male humpback whales sing a complex song consisting of up to ten melodic themes, which are sometimes repeated, all day long. All male humpbacks in the Atlantic Ocean sing the same song, and all male humpbacks in the Pacific Ocean sing the same song, but these two groups sing different songs. No one is sure what the purpose of the song is because the whales do not seem to react to it and because, as I said, the song can go on all day long. This is the extent to which whale behavior exhibits anything like language as far as researchers now know. It has structure and it appears to be innate, but there's no evidence of any of the other four criteria fundamental to language used by humans.

Each Atlantic bottlenose dolphin has a unique whistle, what scientists call a signature. In addition, dolphins use a warning whistle in times of danger to the pod, and each pod of killer whales (which are a type of dolphin, not whale) appears to have a distress call unique to the pod. So when one pod's distress call is recorded and played for another pod, the other pod reacts only with curiosity. This dolphin behavior, then, exhibits structure, appears to be innate, and exhibits limited ability to refer to abstractions (danger). Whether or not it exhibits evidence of cognitive processing depends on whether you think flight or defense reactions to danger of the type practiced by dolphins is reflexive. Regardless, at least two criteria fundamental to human language are absent from dolphin communication.

Some scientists have tried to teach human language to dolphins, just as some have tried to do with birds. Hand gestures that signify objects (such as surfboards, balls, and people), directions (right, left, up, and down), and actions (fetch) are taught to the dolphins, and they are able to respond appropriately. Indeed, they can interpret new utterances correctly. So dolphins who were taught that the sequence of gestures PERSON SURFBOARD FETCH means "bring the surfboard to the person" were able to interpret SURFBOARD PERSON FETCH as "bring the person to the surfboard" without any trouble. Clearly, the dolphins in these experiments recognized structural language rules and exhibited cognitive processing. However, it is still unclear what this tells us about whether or not their own dolphin sounds constitute a language. Also, as with Alex the parrot, what these dolphins do is extremely limited in comparison with how humans manipulate language.

Primates—including chimpanzees, gorillas, bonobos, and others—are the objects of much of the research activity on animal language. Chimpanzees have several types of calls, grunts, barks, pants, wails, laughs, squeaks, and hoots. They use them to alert others to the location of food sources, to announce a successful kill after a hunt, to express alarm at danger or something that strikes them as peculiar, to identify themselves (like the signature whistles of dolphins), and to express satisfaction or peacefulness. Their postures, facial expressions, and limb gestures, however, play a greater role in communication. Yet none of their methods of communication gives evidence of being able to refer to abstract ideas, and no studies have offered any version of a chimpanzee grammar.

On the other hand, some researchers argue that they have taught chimpanzees human language, just as Dr. Pepperberg taught the parrot Alex. However, sign language was used because chimps do not have the physiology that would allow them to produce human language sounds. A chimp named Washoe was immersed in American Sign Language from the age of ten months at the Chimpanzee and Human Communication Institute. When she first saw a swan, she made the signs for WATER and for BIRD. Was she creating a compound word for swan—thus exhibiting a generative language capacity—or was she simply naming the two things she saw? When she was an adult, she was given a baby chimp named Loulis, who she adopted as her son. The scientists did not use ASL around Loulis, but Washoe did, and by the time Loulis was five years old (in 1984), he used 132 reliably identified ASL signs (and there is debate about whether or not he used others). Certainly, the fact that Loulis learned the signs from Washoe could be taken as evidence for an innate language capacity. On the other hand, maybe making the signs was simply a game of mimicry that mother and son played among themselves, for Washoe typically responded to the scientists' use of signs with mimicry.

A female lowland gorilla named Koko was also taught ASL. She amassed a vocabulary of over 1,000 signs, the most of any nonhuman. Koko's use of ASL is among the best-known instances of language experiments with animals. Primary and secondary schools often have videos of Koko signing.

A male bonobo named Kanzi also learned some language, but in a different way. His case was particularly interesting because, like the chimp Loulis, no one tried to teach him language. Instead, the scientists were trying to teach his mother to communicate through a keyboard that had dozens of lexigrams and geometrical designs that represented words. Kanzi picked up the ability to use the keyboard on his own, just from observation, as human children pick up language. Once the scientists recognized what was going on, they actively taught Kanzi, and he acquired an understanding of over 500 spoken English words and about 200 lexigrams. He has shown that he understands rules of grammar, that he can use displacement, and that he can create new sentences. His use of the keyboard, combined with his appropriate behavioral responses to spoken English, certainly look as if he has acquired language, though much more limited language than that of a small child. Again, the evidence suggests that bonobos have the capacity to acquire language, so perhaps they have a language mechanism in the brain, although there is no evidence that they have their own bonobo language.

In my opinion, none of these findings offers convincing evidence that animals use among themselves a natural language that is comparable to human language with respect to the six criteria listed earlier, although bird communication is surprisingly close to the model. Still, studies of animal language have been fewer than studies of human language, and recent studies often debunk false assumptions we've had about animals. For example, most kinds of felines are solitary animals as adults, with the exception of lions. We might expect, then, that if felines had language, lions would be the most likely felines to exhibit it. And, in fact, lions have long been known to use a range of sounds: grunts, moans, puffs, roars, growls, meows (among the cubs), rumbles, and hums. They use these sounds as calls to their young and vice versa, as warnings, as threats, as signs of pleasure, and so on. Often their vocalizations are accompanied by facial expressions, including orientation of the ears, wrinkling of the skin above the nose, widening of the eyes, and lifting of the top lip. In contrast, the solitary tiger has been believed to be nearly silent, making only the occasional cough or roar. But it turns out that tigers roar much more frequently than previously believed, although their roars are very low in pitch, around eighteen Hertz, which is below the frequency band audible to humans. Such a low roar can travel long distances through dense forests. So perhaps tigers are as likely as lions to have or not have language.

Undoubtedly, future studies will uncover other facts about animal communication. But unless these studies yield very different types of results from past studies, it would appear that animal communication is quite different from what we know about language among humans. If animals have the capacity for humanlike language, as in the case of the primates I mentioned, they are not using it among themselves. The capacity for human language is carried by a particular gene: the FoxP2. The FoxP2 protein structures of animals, including other primates, are distinct from those of humans, and it would appear that those distinctions allow for a range of expression suited to needs that are particularly human. Animal communication, on the other hand, may well have complexities that are different from those of human language, needs particular to the different types of animals.

Further Reading

Armstrong, E. 1973. *A study of bird song.* New York: Dover Publications.

Balda, R., I. Pepperberg, and A. Kamil, eds. 1998. *Animal cognition in nature: The convergence of psychology and biology in laboratory and field.* San Diego, Calif.: Academic Press.

Bekoff, M., and D. Jamieson. 1996. *Readings in animal cognition.* Cambridge, Mass.: MIT Press.

Bertram, B. 1978. *Pride of lions.* New York: Scribner.

Bright, M. 1984. *Animal language.* Ithaca, N.Y.: Cornell University Press.

De Luce, J., and H. Wilder, eds. 1983. *Language in primates: Perspectives and implications.* New York: Springer-Verlag.

Findlay, M. 1998. *Language and communication—A cross cultural encyclopedia.* Denver, Colo.: ABC-CLIO.

Griffin, D. 1984. *Animal thinking.* Cambridge, Mass.: Harvard University Press.

Jellis, R. 1977. *Bird sounds and their meaning.* London: British Broadcasting Corporation.

Marler, P. 1980. Birdsong and speech development: Could there be parallels? *American Scientist,* 58: 669–73.

Morton, E., and J. Page. 1992. *Animal talk: Science and the voices of nature.* New York: Random House.

Pinker, S. 1994. *The language instinct: How the mind creates language.* New York: William Morrow.

Rogers, L., and G. Kaplan. 2000. *Songs, roars, and rituals: Communication in birds, mammals, and other animals.* Cambridge, Mass.: Harvard University Press.

Savage-Rumbaugh, S. 1986. *Ape language: From conditioned response to symbol.* New York: Columbia University Press.

Savage-Rumbaugh, S., S. Shanker, and T. Taylor. 1998. *Apes, language, and the human mind.* New York: Oxford University Press.

Sebeok, T., ed. 1968. *Animal communication: Techniques of study and results of research.* Bloomington: Indiana University Press.

———. 1977. *How animals communicate.* Bloomington: Indiana University Press.

Sebeok, T., and R. Rosenthal, eds. 1981. *The clever Hans phenomenon: Communication with horses, whales, apes and people.* New York: New York Academy of Sciences.

Snowdon, C., and M. Hausberger, eds. 1997. *Social influences on vocal development.* New York: Cambridge University Press.

Van Frisch, K. 1971. *Bees, their vision, chemical senses and language.* Ithaca, N.Y.: Cornell University Press.

Web Sites

About chimpanzees: Communication. http://www.janegoodall.org/chimps/chimps_behav_com.html.

Chimpanzee and Human Communication Institute. Frequently asked questions: Signing behavior. http://www.cwu.edu/~cwuchci/main.html

Cyber Zoomobile. Tigers (Pathera tigris). http://www.primenet.com/~brendel/tiger.html

Davies, G. 2001. Bird brains. http://www.pbs.org/lifeofbirds/brain

Gorilla Foundation. Gorilla intelligence and behavior. http://www.gorilla.org/world/

Kaufmann, K. The subject is Alex. http://www.bga.com/~pixel/fun/alex.htm

Language Research Center. Kanzi. http://www.gsu.edu/~wwwlrc/biographies/kanzi.html

Physics Central. Secrets hidden in a tiger's paralyzing roar. http://www.physicscentral.com/news/news-01-1.html

6 Can computers learn language?

As I am writing this book, in 2001, humans can interact verbally with computers in multiple ways. To take a simple example, when I dial the operator at my college and request the campus directory, a recorded voice asks me for the name of the person I'd like to speak to. When I say the name, the recording responds, "Did you say [the name]?" If I respond positively, the phone number of that person is automatically dialed for me. If I respond negatively, the recording apologizes and a human operator comes on the line. Here a voice recognition program is at play. Such programs have been around for quite some time, and they are used in a variety of situations. One of my friends, who has cerebral palsy and is a quadriplegic, has a computer that has been programmed to recognize her voice and make written files of whatever she says. She's used this program for years to type with her voice. There's no doubt, then, that voice recognition by computers is possible.

Therefore, when we hear the common claim that computers can learn language, we might not be skeptical, although we should be. Learning a language is a complex process that involves more than voice recognition. When we ask whether or not computers can learn language, we're asking whether or not we will be able to have conversations with a computer that are indistinguishable from conversations with another person.

People have been asking that question and trying to devise computer programs that will allow a positive answer since as early as 1950, based on the work of Alan Turing, a British mathematician. Turing developed a kind of competition in which an interrogator (by keyboard) tried to figure out which of two respondents was human and which was a computer. He predicted that a computer program would be judged "human" in such a competition within fifty years.

In the 1960s the program ELIZA was developed, which did little more than convert an input statement into a question. The result was that conversations with ELIZA were, jokingly, claimed to resemble conversations with a psychotherapist. Between then and now, there have been other programs. Every time you use a search engine, you engage in a rudimentary kind of conversation with a computer.

If you'd like to try out some current attempts at computer-human conversations, there are at least two that might interest you. One is A.L.I.C.E (http://www.alicebot.org). To any statement or question you input, A.L.I.C.E. responds with a preprogrammed statement or question from her database—and her database is impressively large. Nevertheless, one of my students in the spring of 2001 managed to crash her with the question "How much wood could a woodchuck chuck if a woodchuck could chuck wood?" Another possibility is Daisy (http://www.leedberg.com/glsoft), which is not preprogrammed at all. Rather, Daisy stores your input and manipulates it. So when you first talk with her, she seems to have no intelligence whatsoever (all she can do is repeat what you type in). But if you spend absurdly large amounts of time with her, she gradually comes to form relatively coherent responses.

Despite what seemed to be a reasonable prediction at the time, more than fifty years after Turing made his claim we have not come up with a program that allows a computer to participate like a human in a conversation. Will we ever be able to? At this point, the answer to that question is, of course, speculation. But some guesses are more informed than others. To help you make an informed guess, let's analyze some sample conversations, asking whether or not computers could have produced them. Consider conversation 1:

A. Where are you going?
B. I am going to school.

In thinking about what went into this conversation, we can begin with the most obvious facts. The first fact is that someone produced utterance A. We know computers can produce language—whether preprogrammed (like A.L.I.C.E.) or not (like Daisy)—so A could have been said by a human or a computer.

Response B is based on interpreting utterance A. Again, we know computers can do this to a certain extent. That is, they can analyze sentences to some degree, recognizing verbs, "you" as the subject, and "where" as a location question word. They can then match that sentence with the same verb(s), an appropriate subject, and possible location responses—often responses that begin with "to" (such as "to work," "to the grocery," and in this conversation "to school"). However, if you say the sentences aloud, you will find them stilted. Instead of response B, what would have sounded more natural? Probably this:

C. School.

That is, in casual conversation, we typically answer in fragments rather than in whole sentences. But even if we were to answer in a whole sentence, we wouldn't say, "I am going," but rather the contracted form "I'm going."

These kinds of discrepancies between ordinary and stilted language highlight the fact that spoken language and written language differ. Both forms change over time, but changes in written language usually lag behind changes in spoken language. You might object, saying that response B would be acceptable in conversation if an authority figure had said utterance A. That is, the person who produced response B might be using polite or formal language because of the situation. We exploit these discrepancies in language in our various types of conversation—using more formal styles of language with teachers, employers, and doctors, for example, and less formal ones with siblings, best buddies, and other people from our own age group and background. Computer programs that aim for naturalness must face these issues, which are taken for granted by human speakers.

But these matters do not interfere with comprehension, and if they were the only types of problems computer programs had to face, the outlook for natural computer-human conversations would be good. So let's look at other conversations that raise more thorny problems. Consider conversation 2, which starts with this question:

D. What's up?

Now consider these possible responses (and don't worry about how the question in D would be written):

E. Not much.
F. Got an exam in the morning.
G. Party on Parrish Beach.
H. A preposition.
I. North, of course.
J. Krispy Kreme.

If you're a student, you might answer E, F, G, or a whole range of other possibilities. If you're taking a linguistics class, you could well answer H. If you're standing in front of a wall map, you might answer I. If you're reading the stock page, you could answer J.

In other words, utterances take place within a context. Although sometimes the context imposes only minimally on the response (as in the situation in which a student is basically asking another student if anything special is going on), at other times it allows for only a small range of appropriate answers.

The sensitivity to context covers not just particular situations but also information about cultural habits and facts about nature, mathematics, history, and so on. In short, just about anything can form the relevant context for a conversation. For example:

K. We're getting married, Dad.
L. Honey, come on in here and bring four champagne glasses.

The father is communicating his approval and joy in sentence L by drawing on our knowledge that drinking champagne is a celebratory act.

M. I vomited again this morning.
N. Oh, my god. What's his name?

In interpreting sentence N as an appropriate response to sentence M, we are relying on the fact that morning sickness is often an early sign of pregnancy.

O. He's trying to draw a map of hypothetical countries that requires more than four colors in order to allow every contiguous country to be a different color.
P. The fool.

To see sentence P as a sensible conclusion given sentence O, we're relying on the fact that it is mathematically impossible to need more than four colors to draw such a map.

A computer program that aims for natural conversation must somehow be sensitive to context in all these different ways. These are gigantic problems, and they won't go away, because people move into different places, using their various senses to understand their surroundings. They learn by experiencing the world in a number of ways. The reservoir of their accumulated knowledge feeds their language interactions. Computers, on the other hand, do not gain experiential knowledge that allows them to understand contexts like those above because they don't have senses or cognitive abilities.

We could easily make mobile computers for home and the office; robots are already here, of course. And we could equip them with cameras, so that they have something comparable to vision; tape recorders, so that they have something comparable to hearing; sensors for heat and weight and a variety of other physical characteristics, so that they have something comparable to touch; sensors for various scents, so they have something comparable to smell; and sensors for sweetness, saltiness, acidity, and so forth, so that they have something comparable to taste. If we program in enough information, computers might be able to detect the most common things that human senses detect. But what about the less common ones? What about the nuances, many of which we rely on in understanding our world?

Computers may very well learn, a famous example being the chess-playing computer Deep Blue, which can adapt to new strategies as a chess game progresses. But the ways in which computers learn will limit what they can learn. Deep Blue, for example, can search through millions of possible move sequences, but it is by no means clear whether the heuristics and strategies Deep Blue uses amount to understanding a chess position. It is fast but narrowly limited. Analogous limitations will affect any computer's ability to manipulate language.

You might object that problems involving context are not so much problems of language as problems of communication in general. Perhaps computers would fare better if we limit ourselves to purely linguistic matters. Consider the following examples:

Q. John ate the pie on the windowsill.

Certainly the pie was on the windowsill. But was John also? He might have been. Compare these sentences:

R. John ate his dinner in the restaurant.
S. John ate the candy in that cute little bag.

For sentence R, John was in the restaurant when he ate. For sentence S, John was not in the bag when he ate. A computer must be programmed to allow the prepositional phrase in all these sentences to be analyzed as either modifying the noun that immediately precedes it (yielding the sense in which the noun was in that place but the eating did not occur in that place) or as modifying the verb (yielding the sense that the eating occurred in that place). How does the computer make the choice when it doesn't know what a restaurant is and what a cute little bag is and when it has no knowledge of John's relative size to either of these places? Certainly we could feed the computer a database that notes which words co-occur with which structures, since in the real world there are probabilities associated with situations (people are more likely to eat in restaurants than in bags). But if our sentence were describing a situation with a low probability, the computer would assign the wrong structure, even when a human might well understand the correct structure from the context. Also, if the data base does not happen to cover the relative probabilities of two structures for a given set of words (for example, if we were talking of eating candy with respect to closets), the computer would be at a loss. In that case, we could build in a default structure, since it is likely that one structure occurs with more frequency than the other in general. But the chance of accuracy is only as good as the probability of that structure occuring in general.

It has been estimated that if we considered only sentences with twenty or fewer words in English, we'd have a database of approximately 10^{30} sentences, and many of them could be understood in multiple ways. Consider just this silly little sentence:

T. I saw her duck.

In example T, "I" might have seen an animal or an action, or "I" might be performing the gruesome action of sawing a duck. In some varieties of English, "I" could also have seen a bra strap ("duck" can have that meaning.) And sentence T has only four words. The task with longer sentences is daunting.

Moreover, think about these sentences:

U. Why's Virginia so mad?
V. My sister lost her book.

In response V the sister could have lost her own book or Virginia's book or even some third person's book, although to get this last sense we would probably need some preceding sentences or other context. Contrast sentence V to the possible answer W:

W. My sister lost her cool.

In contrast to sentence V, sentence W has only one interpretation for "her"—my sister. How does the computer recognize this fact?

Commands present additional types of problems. There's a considerable difference between asking a computer to follow a command such as:

X. Tape "The West Wing" at 9 p.m. on Channel 10

and the following command, which my students thought of:

Y. If there's a movie on tonight with Harrison Ford in it, then tape it. But if it's *American Graffiti*, then don't bother because I already have a copy of that.

Whereas I'm optimistic about computers being able to follow command X someday, a command like Y is more difficult. Command X involves activating the record function on a videotape and activating a particular channel at a particular time. It doesn't even ask the computer to scan a list of TV programs. That is, "The West Wing" will be the only program shown at 9 P.M. on Channel 10. However, command Y asks the computer to scan a list of TV programs, recognize which ones are movies, filter out the particular movie *American Graffiti*, determine whether or not Harrison Ford is an actor in the remaining movies, and then activate the record function on a VCR (videocassette recording), at all the appropriate times on all the appropriate channels. These are Boolean tasks, and web search engines perform them all the time. But we feed search engines operators (like "and" and "not") and key vocabulary items that the operators have scope over. In an order like Y, we'd be asking the computer to work from ordinary sentences, extracting the operations and then properly associating them with the correct vocabulary items, a much harder task.

All the issues discussed in this chapter will arise no matter what human language a computer is dealing with. The problems are compounded when we ask computers to deal with more than one language, as in computer translation programs (see chapter 2 for issues in translating). For these reasons, I seriously doubt that people will ever be able to have conversations with computers that are indistinguishable from conversations with humans. I want to leave you with one final conversation, in which I give you a question and a list of possible answers. I leave it to you to think about the difficulties these examples present for computers.

> Question: Why won't you go into that room?
> Answers: Spiders.
>   Superstition.
>   No shoes.
>   No windows.
>   No reason.
>   I won't tell you.
>   Guess.

Further Reading

2000. IEEE International Workshop on Robot and Human Interactive Communication Proceedings. New York: Institute of Electrical & Electronics Engineers, Inc.

Sixth International Conference on Neural Information Processing, 1999. *Minds and machines: Journal for artificial intelligence, philosophy, and cognitive science.* Norwell, Mass.: Kluwer Academic Publishers.

Smith, G. 1991. *Computers and human language.* New York: Oxford University Press.

Web Sites

The Deep Blue team plots its next move. http://www.sciam.com/interview/deepblueinterview.html

A grandmaster chess machine. http://www.sciam.com/explorations/042197chess/042197hsu.html

McCarthy, J. What is artificial intelligence? http://www-formal.
   stanford.edu/jmc/whatisai/whatisai.html

McDermott, D. How intelligent is Deep Blue? http://www.nyu.edu/
   gsas/det/philo/courses/mindsandmachines/m

Meet the players. http://www.research.ibm.com/deepblue/meet/html/
   d.3.html

Neural information processing systems. http://nips.djvuzone.org/
   index.html

Neural information processing systems: Natural and synthetic
   conference, 2001. http://www-2.cs.cmu.edu/Groups/NIPS/

Suber, P. Minds & machines course-related links. Philosophy
   Department, Earlham College, Richmond. Ind. http://www
   .earlham.edu/~peters/courses/mm/mmlinks.htm

Tree-searching techniques. http://www.sciam.com/explorations/
   042197chess/1090hsuB.html

part II
Language in Society

7 Whose speech is better?

Not all speakers of a given language speak the same way. You've noticed speech variations on television. Maybe you've seen the movie *My Fair Lady*, in which Henry Higgins believes that the Queen's English is the superior language of England (and, perhaps, of the world). So the question arises, whose speech is better? And this question is subsumed under the larger question of whether any language is intrinsically superior to another.

Before facing this issue, though, we need to face another matter. Consider these utterances:

> Would you mind if I borrowed that cushion for a few
> moments?
> Could I have that pillow for a sec?
> Give me that, would you?

All of these utterances could be used to request a pillow.

Which one(s) would you use in addressing a stranger? If you use the first one, perhaps you sense that the stranger is quite different from you (such as a much older person or a person with more stature or authority). Perhaps you're trying to show that you're polite or refined or not a threat. Pay attention to the use of the word "cushion" instead of "pillow." Pillows often belong behind our heads, typically in bed. If you wanted to avoid any hint of intimacy, you might choose to use the word "cushion" for what is clearly a pillow.

102 Language in Society

Consider the third sentence. It's harder for some people to imagine using this one with a stranger. When I help to renovate urban housing for the poor with a group called Chester Community Improvement Project and I am pounding in nails next to some guy and sweat is dripping off both our brows, I have no hesitation in using this style sentence. With the informality of such a sentence, I'm implying, or perhaps trying to bring about, a sense of comradery.

Of course, it's easy to imagine a scene in which you could use the second sentence with a stranger.

Which one(s) would you use in addressing someone you know well? Again, it could be all three. But now if you use the first one, you might be insulting the addressee. It's not hard to think of a scenario in which this sentence carries a nasty tone rather than a polite one. And you can describe scenarios for the second and third sentences easily.

The point is that we command different registers of language. We can use talk that is fancy or ordinary or extremely informal, and we can choose which register to use in which situations to get the desired effect. So we have lots of variation in our own speech in the ways we phrase things (syntax) and the words we use (lexicon or vocabulary).

Other variation in an individual's speech involves sound rules (phonology). Say the third sentence aloud several times, playing with different ways of saying it. Contrast "give me" to "gimme" and "would you" to "wudja." When we say words in a sequence, sometimes we contract them, but even a single word can be said in multiple ways. Say the word "interesting" in several sentences, imagining scenarios that differ in formality. Probably your normal (or least marked) pronunciation has three syllables: "in-tres-ting." But maybe it has four, and if it does, they are probably in-er-es-ting."

The pronunciation that is closest to the spelling ("in-ter-es-ting") is more formal and, as a result, is sometimes used for humor (as in "very in-ter-es-ting," with a noticeably foreign flair to the pronunciation of "very" or with a drawn-out "e" in "very").

So you have plenty of variation in your own speech, no matter who you are, and the more different speech communities you belong to, the more variation you will have. With my mother's relatives, I will say, for example, "I hate lobsters anymore," whereas with other people I'm more likely to say, "I hate lobsters these days." This particular use of "anymore" is common to people from certain geographical areas (the North and South Midland, meaning the area from Philadelphia westward through southern Pennsylvania, northern West Virginia, Ohio, Indiana, and Illinois to the Mississsippi River) but not to people from other places, who may not even understand what I mean. With my sister, I used to say, "Ain't nobody gonna tell me what to do," but I'd never say that to my mother or to other people unless I was trying to make a sociolinguistic point. This kind of talk signaled for us a comradery outside of the socioeconomic group my mother aspired to. In a speech to a convention of librarians recently, I said, "That had to change, for I, like you, do not lead a charmed life," but I'd probably never say that in conversation to anyone—it's speech talk. Also, think about the language you use in e-mail and contrast it to your job-related writings, for example.

Although we cannot explicitly state the rules of our language, we do choose to use different rules in different contexts. We happily exploit variation, which we encounter in a wide range, from simple differences in pronunciation and vocabulary to more marked differences that involve phrasing and sentence structure. When the differences are greater and more numerous, we tend to talk of dialects rather than just variations. Thus the languages of upper class and lower class Bostonians would probably be called variations of American English, whereas the languages of upper class and lower class Londoners (Queen's English versus Cockney) would probably be called dialects of British English. When the dialects are so different as to be mutually incomprehensible and/or when they gain a cultural or political status, we tend to talk of separate languages (such as French versus Spanish).

There's one more point I want to make before we return to our original question. I often ask classes to play the game of telephone in the following way. We line up twenty-one chairs, and volunteers sit on them. Then I whisper in the middle person's ear, perhaps something very simple, such as "Come with me to the store." The middle person then whispers the phrase into the ears of people on both sides, and the whisper chain goes on to each end of the line. Finally, the first and twenty-first persons say aloud what they heard.

Next we do the same experiment but this time with a sentence that's a little more tricky, perhaps something such as "Why choose white shoes for winter sports?" Then we do the experiment with a sentence in a language that the first whisperer (who is often not me at this point) speaks reasonably well and might be familiar to some of the twenty-one people in the chairs—perhaps something such as *La lune, c'est magnifique* (which in French means "the moon is wonderful"). Finally, we do the experiment with a sentence whispered initially by a native speaker of a language that none of the twenty-one people speak.

Typically, the first and twenty-first persons do not come up with the same results. Furthermore, the distance between them seems greater with each successive experiment.

Part of the problem is in the listening. We don't all hear things the same way. When we haven't heard something clearly, we ask people to repeat what they said. But sometimes we don't realize we haven't heard something clearly, until our inappropriate response is corrected. At times the other person doesn't correct us and the miscommunication remains, leading to various other difficulties.

Part of the problem in the experiment is in the repeating. You may say, "My economics class is a bore," and you begin the second word with the syllable "eek." I might repeat the sentence but use my pronunciation of the second word, which would begin with "ek." If you speak French well, you might say "magnifique" quite differently from me. In high school or college language classes, the teacher drilled the pronunciation of certain words over and over—but some people never mimicked to her satisfaction. A linguist told me a story about a little girl who introduced herself as "Litha." The man she was introducing herself to said, "Litha?" The child said, "No, Litha." The man said, "Litha?" The child said, "No, no. Litha. Li-tha." The man said, "Lisa?" The child smiled and said, "Right." Repetitions are not exact and lead to change.

Imperfections in hearing and repeating are two of the reasons that language must change over time. When the Romans marched into Gaul and into the Iberian peninsula and northeastward into what is now Romania, they brought large populations who stayed and spoke a form of street Latin. But over time, the street Latin in Gaul developed into French; that in the Iberian Peninsula developed into Portuguese along the west and Spanish along the east and central portions; that in Romania developed into Romanian. Moreover, the street Latin spoken in the original community on the Italian peninsula changed as well, developing into Italian.

Other factors (besides our imperfections in hearing and in repeating sounds) can influence the speed with which language changes and the ways in which it changes—but the fact is that living languages necessarily change. They always have and they always will.

Many political groups have tried to control language change. During the French Revolution, a controlling faction decided that a standard language would pave the way for unity. Parish priests, who were ordered to survey spoken language, found that many dialects were spoken in different geographic areas, and many of them were quite distinct from the dialect of Paris. Primary schools in every region of France were established with teachers proficient in the Parisian dialect. The effect of this educational reform was not significant until 1881, when state education became free and mandatory, and the standard dialect (that is, Parisian) took hold more firmly. Still, the geographic dialects continued, though weakened, and most important, the standard kept changing. Standard French today is different from the Parisian dialect of 1790. In addition, new varieties of French have formed, as new subcultures have appeared. Social dialects persist and/or arise even when geographic dialects are squelched. Change is the rule in language, so variation will always be with us.

Now we can ask whose speech is better. This is a serious question because our attitudes about language affect how we treat speakers in personal, as well as in business and professional, situations. In what follows I will use the term "standard American English" (a term riddled with problems, which will become more and more apparent as you read)—the variety that we hear in news reports on television and radio. It doesn't seem to be strongly associated with any particular area of the country, although those who aren't from the Midwest often call it midwestern. This variety is also more frequently associated with the middle class than with the lower class, and it is more frequently associated with whites than with other races.

A few years ago a white student from Atlanta, Georgia, recorded herself reading a passage of James Joyce both in standard

American English pronunciation and in her Atlanta pronunciation. She then asked strangers (adults of varying ages who lived in the town of Swarthmore, Pennsylvania) to listen to the two readings and answer a set of questions she had prepared. She did not tell the strangers that the recordings were made by a single person (nor that they were made by her). Without exception, the strangers judged the person who read the passage with standard English pronunciation as smarter and better educated, and most of them judged the person who read the passage with Atlanta pronunciation as nicer and more laid-back. This was just a small, informal study, but its findings are consistent with those of larger studies.

Studies have shown that prejudice against certain varieties of speech can lead to discriminatory practices. For example, Professor John Baugh of Stanford University directed a study of housing in which he used different English pronunciations when telephoning people who had advertised apartments for rent. In one call he would use standard American pronunciation; in another, African-American; in another, Latino. (He is African American, but he grew up in the middle class in Los Angeles with many Latino friends. He can sound white, African American, or Latino, at will.) He said exactly the same words in every call, and he controlled for the order in which he made the calls (i.e., sometimes the Latino pronunciation would be used first, sometimes the African-American, and sometimes the standard). He asked if the apartments were still available. More were available when he used the standard pronunciation. Thus it is essential that we examine carefully the question of "better" with regard to language variety.

When I knock on a door and my friend inside says, "Who's there?" I'm likely to answer, "It's me," but I don't say, "It's I" (or, even more unlikely for me, "It is I"). Do you? If you do, do you say that naturally, that is, not self-consciously? Or do you say it because you've been taught that that's the correct thing to say? If you do it naturally, your speech contains an archaism—a little fossil from the past. We all have little fossils. I say, "I'm different from you." Most people today would say, "I'm different than you." My use of "from" after "different" was typical in earlier generations, but it's not typical today. Some of us hold onto archaisms longer than others, and even the most linguistically innovative of us probably have some. So don't be embarrassed by your fossils: They're a fact of language.

But if you say "It's I" self-consciously because you've been taught that that's correct, what does "correct" mean in this situation? If that's what most people used to say but is not what most people say today, you're saying it's correct either because you revere the past (which many of us do) or because you believe that there's a rule of language that's being obeyed by "It's I" and being broken by "It's me."

I'm going to push the analysis of just this one contrast—"It's I" versus "It's me"—quite a distance because I believe that many relevant issues about how people view language will come out of the discussion. Consider the former reason for preferring "It's I," that of revering the past. Many people have this reason for using archaic speech patterns and for preferring that others use them. For some reason, language is treated in a unique way here. We certainly don't hold up the past as superior in other areas, for example, mathematics or physics. So why do some of us feel that changes in language are evidence of decay?

If it were true that the older way of saying something were better simply because it's older, your grandparents spoke better than your parents and your great-grandparents spoke better than your grandparents and so on. Did Chaucer speak a form of English superior to that spoken by Shakespeare? Shall we go further back

prejudice is a reality. The adult who cannot speak and write the standard variety may encounter a range of difficulties, from finding suitable employment to achieving social advancement.

At the same time, all of us—and educational institutions, in particular—should respect all varieties of language and show that respect in relevant ways. Look at one notorious controversy: In 1996 the school board in Oakland, California, declared Ebonics to be the official language of the district's African-American students. Given funding regulations for bilingual education in that time and place, this decision had the effect of allowing the school district to use funds set aside for bilingual education to teach their African-American children in Ebonics, as well as in the standard language.

The debate was particularly hot, I believe, because of the sociological issues involved. Many people thought that Ebonics should be kept out of the classroom purely because the dialect was associated with race. Some of these people were African Americans who did not want their children to be disadvantaged by linguistic prejudice; they were afraid that teaching in Ebonics would exaggerate racial linguistic prejudice rather than redress it. Many good books written about the Ebonics controversy for the general public look at the issue from a variety of perspectives (see the suggested readings). But from a linguistic perspective, the issue is more a question of bilingual (or bi-dialectal) education than anything else. If you care about the Ebonics issue, I urge you to read chapter 11, keeping Ebonics in mind.

In sum, variation in language is something we all participate in, and, as a linguist and a writer, I believe it's something we should revel in. Language is not a monolith, nor can it be, nor should it be, given the complexity of culture and the fact that language is the fabric of culture. Some of us are more eloquent than others, and all of us have moments of greater or lesser eloquence. But that range in eloquence is found in every language, every dialect, and every variety of speech.

Further Reading on Variation

Andersson, L. G., and P. Trudgill. 1990. *Bad language*. Cambridge: Blackwell.

Baron, D. 1994. *Guide to home language repair*. Champaign, Ill.: National Council of Teachers of English.

Baugh, J. 1999. *Out of the mouths of slaves*. Austin: University of Texas Press.

Biber, D., and E. Finegan. 1997. *Sociolinguistic perspectives on register*. Oxford: Oxford University Press.

Cameron, D. 1995. *Verbal hygiene*. London: Routledge.

Carver, C. 1989. *American regional dialects: A word geography*. Ann Arbor: University of Michigan Press.

Coulmas, F. 1998. *Handbook of sociolinguistics*. Cambridge: Blackwell.

Fasold, R. 1984. *The sociolinguistics of society*. New York: Blackwell.

Finegan, E. 1980. *Attitudes toward language usage*. New York: Teachers College Press.

Fishman, J. 1968. *Readings in the sociology of language*. Paris: Mouton.

Herman, L. H., and M. S. Herman. 1947. *Manual of American dialects for radio, stage, screen, and television*. New York: Ziff Davis.

Hock, H., and B. Joseph. 1996. *An introduction to historical and comparative linguistics*. Berlin: Mouton de Gruyter.

Labov, W. 1972. *The logic of nonstandard English in language and social context: Selected readings*. Compiled by Pier Paolo Giglioli. Baltimore Md.: Penguin.

———. 1972. *Sociolinguistic patterns*. Philadelphia: University of Pennsylvania Press.

LeClerc, F., Schmitt, B. H., and Dube, L. 1994, May. Foreign branding and its effects on product perceptions and attitudes. *Journal of Marketing Research*, 31: 263–270.

Lippi-Green, R. 1997. *English with an accent*. New York: Routledge.

McCrum, R., W. Cran, and R. MacNeil. 1986. *The story of English*. New York: Viking Penguin.

Millward, C. M. 1989. *A biography of the English language*. Orlando, Fla.: Holt, Rinehart and Winston.

Milroy, J., and L. Milroy. 1991. *Authority in language*, 2nd ed. London: Routledge.

Moss, B., and K. Walters. 1993. Rethinking diversity: Axes of difference in the writing classroom. In L. Odell, ed., *Theory and practice in the teaching of writing: Rethinking the discipline*. Carbondale: Southern Illinois University Press.

Peyton, J,, S. McGinnis, and D. Ranard, eds. 2001. *Heritage languages in America: Preserving a national resource* (from Delta Systems, phone 800–323–8270), Arlington, Va.

Romaine, S. 1994. *Language in society: An introduction to sociolinguistics*. Oxford: Oxford University Press.

Scherer, K., and H. Giles, eds. 1979. *Social markers in speech*. New York: Cambridge University Press.

Seligman, C. R., G. R. Tucker, and W. Lambert. 1972. The effects of speech style and other attributes on teachers' attitudes toward pupils. *Language and Society*, 1: 131–42.

Trask, R. L. 1994. *Language change*. London: Routledge.

Weinreich, U. [1953] 1968. *Languages in contact*. The Hague: Mouton.

Wolfram, W. 1991. *Dialects and American English*. Englewood Cliffs, N.J.: Prentice Hall.

Wolfram, W., and N. Schilling-Estes. 1998. *American English–dialects and variation*. Oxford: Blackwell.

Web Sites

Center for Applied Linguistics—Sources on Dialects.
http://www.cal.org/topics/dialres.htm

Hazen, K. (ongoing—accessed April 2001). Variety is the spice of life.
http://www.as.wvu.edu/~khazen/WVDP.HTML

Labov, W. How I got into linguistics, and what I got out of it.
    http://www.ling.upenn.edu/~labov/Papers/HowIgot.html
Thomason, S. Language variation and change.
    http://www.lsadc.org/web2/variation.html
University of Oregon—Explore linguistics and sociolinguistics.
    http://logos.uoregon.edu/explore/socioling/
University of Pennsylvania—Can reading failure be reversed?
    http://www.ling.upenn.edu/phono_atlas/RFR.html
University of Pennsylvania—Phonological atlas of North America.
    http://www.ling.upenn.edu/phono_atlas/home.html

Further Reading on Ebonics

Adger, C. 1994. Enhancing the delivery of services to black spe-
    cial education students from non-standard English back-
    grounds. Final Report. University of Maryland, Institute for
    the Study of Exceptional Children and Youth. (Available
    through ERIC Document Reproduction Service. Document
    No. ED 370 377.)
Adger, C., D. Christian, and O. Taylor. 1999. *Making the connection:*
    Language and academic achievement among African American
    students. Washington, D.C. and McHenry, Ill.: Center for
    Applied Linguistics and Delta Systems.
Adger, C., W. Wolfram, and J. Detwyler. 1993. Language differences:
    A new approach for special educators. *Teaching Exceptional*
    Children, 26, no. (1): 44–47.
Adger, C., W. Wolfram, J. Detwyler, and B. Harry. 1993. Confronting
    dialect minority issues in special education: Reactive and
    proactive perspectives. In *Proceedings of the Third National*
    Research Symposium on Limited English Proficient Student Issues:
    Focus on Middle and High School Issues, 2: 737–62. U.S. Depart-
    ment of Education, Office of Bilingual Education and Minority
    Languages Affairs. (Available through ERIC Document Repro-
    duction Service. Document No. ED 356 673.)

Baratz, J. C., and R. W. Shuy, eds. 1969. Teaching black children to read. Available as reprints from the Univrsity of Michigan, Ann Arbor (313–761–4700).

Baugh, J. 2000. *Beyond Ebonics*. New York: Oxford University Press.

Christian, D. 1997. Vernacular dialects and standard American English in the classroom. ERIC Minibib. Washington, D.C.: ERIC Clearinghouse on Languages and Linguistics. (This minibibliography cites seven journal articles and eight documents related to dialect usage in the classroom. The documents can be accessed on microfiche at any institution with the ERIC collection, or they can be ordered directly from EDRS.)

Dillard, J. L. 1972. *Black English: Its history and use in the U.S.* New York: Random House.

Fasold, R. W. 1972. Tense marking in black English: A linguistic and social analysis. Available as reprints from the University of Michigan, Ann Arbor (313–761–4700).

Fasold, R. W., and R. W. Shuy, eds. 1970. *Teaching standard English in the inner city*. Washington, D.C.: Center for Applied Linguistics.

Wiley, T. G. 1996. The case of African American language. In *Literacy and language diversity in the United States*, pp. 125–32. Washington, D. C.: Center for Applied Linguistics and Delta Systems.

Wolfram, W. 1969. A sociolinguistic description of Detroit Negro speech. Available as reprints from the University of Michigan, Ann Arbor (313–761–4700).

——— 1990, February. Incorporating dialect study into the language arts class. *ERIC Digest*. Available from the ERIC Clearinghouse on Languages and Linguistics, Center for Applied Linguistics, 4646 40th Street NW, Washington, D.C. 20016–1859, (202–362–0700).

———. 1994. Bidialectal literacy in the United States. In D. Spener, ed., *Adult biliteracy in the United States*, pp. 71–88. Washington, D.C.: Center for Applied Linguistics and Delta Systems.

Wolfram, W., and C. Adger. 1993. *Handbook on language differences and speech and language pathology: Baltimore City public schools.* Washington, D.C.: Center for Applied Linguistics.

Wolfram, W., C. Adger, and D. Christian. 1999. Dialects in schools and communities. Mahwah, N.J.: Erlbaum.

Wolfram, W., and N. Clarke, eds. 1971. *Black-white speech relationships.* Washington, D.C.: Center for Applied Linguistics.

8 Why do dialects and creoles differ from standard language?

Misunderstandings of dialect diversity and of creoles have led to common claims that some languages are deficient, revealing carelessness or even stupidity. Indeed, language discrimination is tolerated by people who would never tolerate discriminatory remarks based on race, ethnicity, gender, sexual orientation, or many other characteristics. The goal of this chapter is to understand what dialects and creoles are, so that such misconceptions can be erased. Along the way we will face an astonishing fact about creoles, one that has been pivotal in the understanding of the human mind.

In chapter 7, we saw that language changes over time. This is a hard-and-fast rule. Some language communities are highly innovative linguistically, and over several hundred years the changes in their language might be drastic; other language communities are linguistically conservative, and the changes might be minimal. But over time there will be changes in any language.

In chapter 7 we also noted two factors that contribute to bringing about language change: We do not all hear the same way, and we do not all repeat exactly what we've heard. But many other factors can be relevant to language change. One of the most important is contact with other languages.

American society is quite fluid, and families and individuals move from place to place often. These moves have linguistic effects on individuals, although they are usually minimal, particularly on adults. They do not have effects on the overall language community that a person or family moves into.

My oldest daughter was born in Boston but we moved to Chapel Hill, North Carolina, when she was six weeks old. When she was a year old, we moved to Washington, D.C., and lived in Mount Pleasant, a racially and ethnically mixed neighborhood, where her best friends spoke Korean, the Spanish of El Salvador, and African-American English. She went to a public nursery program for three-year-olds in which all the other children but two were African American (one spoke German, one Korean.) She then went to a public bilingual prekindergarten and then a kindergarten in which all the other children but one were native speakers of Spanish. When she was six, we moved to Ann Arbor, Michigan, and she went to a public elementary school. Although classes were held in English, about half the students were children of foreign graduate students at the University of Michigan. Her two best friends' native languages were Swedish and Japanese. When she was thirteen, we moved to Swarthmore, Pennsylvania, to a linguistically unremarkable school district. She studied Spanish and Latin all through high school. She then went to Durham, North Carolina, for college, where she studied Italian, and then to Philadelphia, Pennsylvania for medical school. She now lives in Manhattan. During the first twenty-two years of her life, she heard English at home but spent most of her summers in various parts of Italy.

If you heard my daughter Elena speak, I doubt you could guess the richness of her exposure to other languages and to multiple varieties of English. When we first came to Swarthmore, her friends would correct her for saying "pop" instead of "soda," and she pronounced the word "egg" with the same vowel that starts the word "ate" in standard English—but that changed. Although she never picked up a Philadelphia pronunciation, she no longer has any traces of a midwestern one. I would bet that someone trained in regional variations of American English would have a lot of trouble pegging her speech. All her exposure has somehow leveled out a lot of regional characteristics that she might have had if she had grown up in Chapel Hill, Washington, D.C., or Ann Arbor.

That's true of many of us: The more places we've lived in for a considerable period, the more likely our language will be somewhat sanitized of regional characteristics. But the important point is that wherever Elena went, none of her friends picked up from her any linguistic characteristics of the language community she had recently moved from. That is, Elena did not influence Ann Arborites to speak with a Washington, D.C., accent, nor Swarthmoreans to speak with an Ann Arborite accent. Elena's story is typical; the language of isolated individuals does not tend to have effects on language communities.

If, on the other hand, 30,000 people from our neighborhood in Washington, D.C., had moved to Ann Arbor (a town of only 60,000 inhabitants at the time) and if they had stayed through a few generations, there might have been noticeable linguistic influences from the newcomers on the language of the Ann Arborites. And if 3,000 people from Ann Arbor had moved to Swarthmore (a town that has about 6,000 inhabitants, including 1,350 students at the local college) and if they had stayed through a few generations, there might have been some suspiciously midwestern ways of saying things at the local schools.

Large migrations of people do happen, of course. Sometimes the migrating people are more populous than the indigenous people, and the language of the immigrants supplants that of the latter. That happened when the British colonized Australia: indigenous languages of Australia were all but wiped out. (The most populous Aboriginal language community, which speaks Walpiri, has a little over 200 speakers as of the writing of this book.) Of course, the English spoken in Australia changed over time and diversified regionally, so Australians can tell whether someone comes from Perth, Melbourne, Darwin, or so on. Australian varieties of English are now quite distinct from British varieties (as well as American, Canadian, Indian, etc.). However, standard Australian English is quite mutually comprehensible with standard British English and standard American English—so we tend to call them all dialects rather than separate languages.

What's the difference between a dialect and a variety? From a linguistic point of view it might be the extent of the linguistic differences between the two ways of talking, in that two dialects have less in common than two varieties of a language. However, in common talk, it's largely a sociological and political matter. If a group of people sees itself as distinct from another group (distinct in any number of ways, including culture, politics, race, sexual orientation, etc.), these people may prefer to talk about dialects rather than varieties of a language.

Now there is a set of dialects. As time goes on, though, these dialects might change enough so that they are no longer mutually comprehensible. At that point, they probably have different governments and we would probably call them separate languages rather than dialects. English and German are such languages. That is, Germanic tribes settled in England, and both the immigrants' language and the original Old German of the tribes left behind on the mainland changed—each in separate and independent ways, with the result that English and German today are not mutually comprehensible. The fact that they share a somewhat close ancestor (what we'd call Proto-Germanic) means that they are genetically related—sister languages that belong to the Germanic family (which also includes Dutch and Flemish and the Scandinavian languages of Norwegian, Swedish, Icelandic, and Danish, as well as Africaans, a daughter of Dutch).

But migrating people do not always wipe out or displace the indigenous languages. Sometimes the former coexist with the indigenous people in such a way that both languages continue to be spoken. If the migrating people are numerous enough and stay long enough, their language can have serious linguistic effects on the entire community's language, to the point that the resulting language has a lot in common with both the previous languages. That happened when the Normans marched into England in 1066 and stayed. Old English was a Germanic language; Norman was a French dialect (French is in the Romance family). Over many generations, the language of the Normans influenced every aspect of the structure of English, so that today English is a highly Frenchified Germanic language.

You can see the mixed heritage of English all through the vocabulary. English has the Germanic word "tooth" beside the Romance root "dent-" (in "dental"); the Germanic word "hound" beside the Romance root "can-" (in "canine"); the Germanic word "laugh" beside the Romance root "rid" (in "ridicule"). Can you see the pattern? In general, the short words are Germanic and the roots that must be part of longer words (so called bound roots) are Romance. The Germanic words tend to feel ordinary or crude or tough, whereas the words based on Romance roots tend to feel a little more special or refined or delicate. That's true even when the Romance words are short. So "calf" is a Germanic word, and it's used for the animal. But "veal" is a Romance word, and it's used for the meat of the animal—as though by using the Romance name, we can see the meat as somehow different from that little animal in the barnyard. Speakers feel this difference even in slang today. Compare the impact of Germanic "mother" to the Romance "mamma" in these two casual utterances by (unenlightened) young men, looking at passing women:

> Boy, is she a mother.
> Boy, is she a mamma.

Which term do you think these hypothetical young men would use for a woman they found really attractive? Which would they use for a woman they found totally unattractive? Do you see a distinction? Some people say that "mamma" is more likely for the woman they consider attractive, probably because the Normans were the rulers—with all the riches and the things wealth buys at their disposal—so their speech became associated with the upper class and with good things in general.

However, a much more common situation is one in which a language community comes in contact with another to varying degrees, but not nearly so extensively as the Normans in England. In cases of relatively limited or brief language contact (perhaps a generation or two), the visiting language will have little effect on the indigenous language, and one typically limited to vocabulary. Languages are relatively quick to borrow vocabulary, slower to borrow pronunciation, and slowest to borrow rules of word formation and of sentence structure. Thus many dialects of Spanish in the south of Spain, in particular, have words of Arabic origin because of the invasions of the Moors, but their word formation and sentence structure are Spanish. Other examples of this sort of situation are easy to come by.

A very different situation can arise, however. Let's say that two groups of people have to communicate with each other because they must conduct business together. Let's also say that they do not have a language in common and their two languages are quite distinct from each other. Finally, let's assume that one of the languages belongs to people who have a lot of authority behind them in this situation, whereas the other does not. For example, one language might be French and the other might be a (mix of) language(s) of African slaves—a situation that arose in Haiti. Or one language might be English and the other might be a (mix of) language(s) of Papua New Guinea—another real situation. What do you think will happen?

What would you do if you were put in a room with someone who spoke Japanese; the two of you did not share any language, and the Japanese person had to work for you in getting a particular job done? (In other words, you are the one with the authority.) You'd probably resort to gestures and pointing but quickly discover that impromptu gestures have severe limitations in communicative possibilities. Thus you'd want to use language. You're the one with the authority, so probably you'd prefer teaching the other person some English words for some of the tools, rather than learning the Japanese words. Perhaps you'd also name the pieces of the machine you're putting together and various other items you have to refer to, as well as a few actions, so that you're ready to work.

But now that you've got some words in common, how do you put them together? There's a lot more to language than a set of words. Are you going to say, "Would you please pick up the second wrench on your left right away and tighten this bolt while I hold the chassis in place?" This sentence has too many words and too complex a structure. Which words have meanings that you must absolutely convey? Perhaps these are "pick up," "second," "wrench," "left," "right away," "tight," and "bolt." Perhaps you'll use "get" instead of "pick up," for simplicity's sake. You may repeat "fast" rather than say "right away" for the same reason, and the whole idea of "while I hold the chassis in place" might not even be necessary. Therefore, you may try stringing together these key words: "Get second wrench, left, fast fast, tight bolt." It sounds dreadful but might be effective, even though it is missing a lot of the connective tissue of language.On the other hand, it does have normal English word order.

If the Japanese person were to try to convey that same information to you, using the same words, she might say something like this: "Bolt tight, fast fast left second wrench get." Verbs come at the end of a sentence in Japanese.

The bare-bones contact language you and the Japanese person were creating is called a pidgin. Pidgins arise often and all over the world. The language of the authority figure is typically called the superstratum, the other language the substratum. The pidgin tends to have the vocabulary of the superstratum but the sentence structure of the substratum. Why? Generally, there isn't a one-on-one situation. There might be a hundred people working for a single authority figure. You know, from the discussion of dialects, that language communities are quick to borrow vocabulary but slow to accept innovations in sentence structure. So the substratum, which typically has more speakers, determines the sentence structure of the pidgin. Still, individual speakers of a pidgin might employ their own private methods for putting sentences together. In fact, both the pronunciation and the sentence structure are highly unstable from speaker to speaker.

Here's a real sentence from a Japanese-English pidgin (http://grove.afl.edu/~jodibray/LIN3010/Study_Aids/pidgin.htm):

da pua pipl awl poteto it.
the poor people only potatoes eat
"The poor people ate only potatoes."

Here's another real sentence from a Philipino-English pidgin (from the same Web site):

wok had dis pipl
work hard these people
"These people work hard."

As you might guess, the verb comes in the beginning of the sentence of the substratum Philipino language (Tagalog).

Pidgins are special languages in that they have no native speakers. Everyone who speaks a pidgin also speaks his or her native language.

Pidgins often come into existence when the right kind of contact situation arises and go out of existence when that situation dissipates, but sometimes the situation prevails for a long time. In that case, children are born into the pidgin-speaking community. They are exposed to the pidgin from the beginning, making their linguistic situation unique.

One of the most marvelous facts discovered by linguists is that the very first generation of children born into a pidgin-speaking community develops its own language, called a creole, which has vocabulary in common with the pidgin but a set of rules for sentence formation that is not derivative from either the superstratum or the substratum. The rules that creoles exhibit are found in many languages that are not creoles—they are natural rules of language. But the most amazing fact of all is that creoles around the world, regardless of their superstratum and substratum, have much in common with one another. There are over one hundred creoles in the world, so their common characteristics cannot simply be accidental. Before the technological advances that allowed for brain imaging and other kinds of experimental work and before the discovery of the gene FoxP2, the structure of creoles was one of the strongest pieces of evidence for the existence of a language mechanism in the brain.

Typical characteristics of creoles include the following:

1. Creoles tend to have simplified vowel systems, often having only five vowels. In contrast, standard American English (for a discussion of the notion of "standard," read chapter 7), for example, has twelve vowels. This claim might surprise you since we identify only five letters of the Roman alphabet as vowels, but English distinguishes twelve vowel sounds. Say these words:

> bat, bet, bait, bit, beat

There are five different vowel sounds here (and two of them might well be lengthened in a particular way called a diphthong). Now say these words:

> cod, cawed (as in the sound of a crow), code, could, cooed
> (as in the sound of a dove)

There are five vowel sounds here (again, two of them might well be lengthened in a variety of English), and they are distinct from the vowel sounds in the first list of words. Now say these two words:

> but, gallop

The vowel sound in "but" and the vowel sound in the second syllable of "gallop" are probably distinct from any of the vowel sounds in the other two word lists—which is what I mean when I say that American English has twelve vowels.

The five vowels that many creoles have are typically (similar to) those found in the English words:

> cod, bait, beat, code, cooed

2. Creoles tend to have a relatively restricted vocabulary, although it is much more extensive than that of the pidgin. Never-

theless, words are used for a range of meanings in a creole, and everything people need to express is expressable, just as it is in any other natural human language. Notice that any language uses the same words for many meanings. Compare the (partial) range of senses that "run" has:

I run to the store.
Those stockings run too easily.
You can't run such a complicated business.
We run ourselves crazy with too much to do.
Rivers run downhill.
Children's noses run in the winter.
But our cars never run in the winter.

Just for fun, make your own list of the (partial) range of senses that "give" has.

3. Creoles tend to express variations in time by having a string of helping verbs rather than by having complicated word formation rules. In other words, they are more like English in this respect than like a language such as Italian:

English: I thought she might have been sleeping.
Italian: Pensavo che dormisse.

The idea of potential (in the English "might"), completed or whole action (in the English "have"), and stretched-out activity (in the English "been") that go with "sleeping" are all expressed in the ending on the Italian verb *dormisse*. (*Dorm* is the root for "sleep"; *isse* is the ending that carries all the meaning about the time frame.) Here's an example from Hawaiian Creole English (www.ac.wwu.edu/~sngynan/sbc3.html):

George been stay go play.
"George might have been playing."

4. Creoles tend to express negation by placing a negative word immediately in front of the first verb. The example below is from Rarotongan, a Maori-English creole, spoken on one of the Cook Islands:

Jou no kamu ruki me.
you—not—have—look—me
"You have not seen me."

5. Creoles tend to place the verb between the subject and the object (as English does) and as in the above example from Rarotongan).

Creoles are spoken all over the world. The superstrata of most creoles are European languages, although there are creoles in which the superstratum is an American Indian language (Chinook, Delaware, or Mobilian), Arabic, Malay, Swahili, Zulu, and so on. Because of the way in whichcreoles originate, they are often considered substandard languages, although linguistically there is nothing substandard about them. The creole Tok Pisin has, in fact, become the official national language of Papua New Guinea.

The situations under which languages come in contact with one another vary enormously, and the effects of language contact vary accordingly. Language contact is undoubtedly one of the most important factors in language change, one that can bring about striking and radical changes, sometimes in a short period of time (as with creoles). Just as undoubtedly, change will occur even when a language is isolated from other languages.

Further Reading

Appel, R., and P. Muysken. 1987. *Language contact and bilingualism.* London: Edward Arnold.

Arends, J., P. Muysken, and N. Smith, eds. 1995. *Pidgins and creoles: An introduction.* Amsterdam: John Benjamins.

Bickerton, D. 1981. *Roots of Language.* Ann Arbor, Mich.: Karoma.

Cable, G. W. [1884] 1970. *The creoles of Louisiana.* New York: Scribner's.

Görlach, M. 1991. *Englishes: Studies in varieties of English 1984–1988.* Amsterdam: John Benjamins.

Holm, J. 1988–89. *Pidgins and creoles,* 2 vol. Cambridge: Cambridge University Press.

Myers-Scotton, C. 1993. *Social motivations for codeswitching: Evidence from Africa.* Oxford: Clarendon.

Romaine, S. 1988. *Pidgin and creole languages.* New York: Longman.

———. 1989. *Bilingualism.* Oxford: Basil Blackwell.

———. 1994. *Language in society.* Oxford: Oxford University Press.

Sebba, M. 1997. *Contact languages: Pidgins and creoles.* New York: St. Martin's.

Thomason, S., and T. Kaufmann. 1988. *Language contact, creolization and genetic linguistics.* Berkeley: University of California Press.

Todd, L. 1990. *Pidgins and creoles.* London: Routledge.

Weinreich, U. 1953. *Languages in contact: Findings and problems,* 2nd ed. The Hague: Mouton.

Web Sites

Cajuns and creoles . . . creoles and cajuns. http://www.neworleansweb.org/cajun.html

Krelerak/Creoles. http://www.geocities.com/Athens/9479/kreole.html

Language family trees: Creole. http://www.ethnologue.com/show_family.asp?name=Creole&subid=140

Language miniatures. http://home.bluemarble.net/~langmin/

Lecture on creoles. http://www.ac.wwu.edu/~sngynan/slx3.html

Numbers in pidgins, creoles, and constructed languages. http://www.zompist.com/last.htm

Pidgins. http://grove.ufl.edu/~jodibray/LIN3010/Study_Aids/pidgin.htm

Pidgins and creoles. http://babel.uoregon.edu/romance/rl407/creole/
    creole.html, http://logos.uoregon.edu/explore/socioling/pidgin.
    html, http://www.ac.wwu.edu/~sngynan/discuss3.html, and http:
    //www.anthro.mnsu.edu/cultural/language/pidgcreol.html
Post-contact languages of western Australia. http://coombs.anu.edu
    .au/WWWVLPages/AborigPages/LANG/WA/4_7.htm
Tok Pisin: The national language of Papua New Guinea. http://www
    .siu.edu/departments/cola/ling/reports/Etepa/
Words & stuff: cc: pidgin carriers. http://www.kith.org/logos/words/
    upper2/CCreole.html

9 Do men and women talk differently? And who cares?

In earlier chapters, I discussed three important factors that influence language change: the fact that people don't all hear the same (chapter 7), the fact that people don't all repeat in the same way (also chapter 7), and contact among different languages (chapter 8). But even if there were a linguistic community in which people actually did all hear and repeat language in the same way and even if that community were monolingual and totally isolated from other linguistic communities, its language would change over time because other factors influence language change, factors internal to a society. In this chapter we'll look at the interaction of gender roles and language, but first let's briefly face a larger question.

Why do social factors bring about language change? There are many theories, but they tend to boil down to one basic concept. Imagine that we live in a society in which everyone dresses the same. How long do you think this will continue? Not too long—someone is going to shorten a hem, roll up a T-shirt sleeve (carrying a little pad of Post-its in the newly created pocket), use a shawl as a festive skirt, or keep wearing jeans long after the threadbare stage. Even if most of us ignore the change, some might copy it, and sometimes most of us will copy it. If enough of us do so, of course, it's no longer a daring thing to do. It becomes the new status quo, and then we wait for another iconoclast.

People experiment with language and thus bring about language change, just as they experiment with hemlines and bring about style change. The interesting difference, however, is that language does not change in arbitrary ways but rather in ways that conform to general principles. As native speakers of our language, we do not have a conscious and explicit knowledge of these principles, just as we don't have an explicit knowledge of the process of metabolism of sugar (except for the chemists among us). Nevertheless, we adhere to those principles, and if our pancreas is healthy, we metabolize sugar.

What are these principles? Let me give a small example. Several years ago, it was popular among young people to say a sentence and then put a negative at the end, a kind of sarcasm. For example, if you had asked your teenage son what he was going to do after dinner on a Friday night, he might have said, "I'm going to be studying for hours . . . not." This usage was widespread, and I wondered at a certain point if it might actually become part of American English sentence structure. Putting a marker (like "not") at the beginning or end of an utterance that the marker relates to (or, as linguists and philosophers would say, "operates over") is common in language. Some Chinese questions can be structurally identical to statements, for example, the only difference being the presense of a question marker (*ma*) at the end. Thus the English negative structure was not in violation of any general linguistic principles. It did not, in fact, last long, but the point is that it could have.

On the other hand, if someone had ever tried to introduce a negative structure such as "I am not going not not to be not not not studying not not not not for hours," it would never have had a chance of catching on. What I did here was to add after the verb form the number of "not"s that corresponded to its position in the sentence. So the first verb form, "am," had one "not" after it. The second, "going," had two, and so on. Why is this structure so strange from a linguistic point of view? It seems that language principles do not allow counting linguistic units beyond three at most, whether in the sound system, the word formation system, the sentence structure system, or the meaning system. We are hard-wired not to do it. (Most of the chapters in part I should convince you that it makes sense to talk about being hard-wired for language.)

Let's return to our linguistically isolated and homogenously monolingual community. Someone introduces a language change that does adhere to general linguistic principles. Which potential changes actually endure and become the new status quo? It is impossible to predict. Languages often look as if they are heading in a certain linguistic direction and then change course. No reputable linguist will predict language change.

Still, we know that certain factors are important in language change within a linguistic community: race, ethnicity, social class, educational background, age, and gender, among others. Much has been written about these factors (and others), but that material is usually aimed at linguistic scholars. An exception is gender: Quite a lot has been written for the general public about the male and female use of language, particularly conversational behavior. The question of whether men and women talk differently is at least as important to the general public as any other question about gender roles, and it is arguably more important because language is such an intrinsic part of our identities.

The first step in answering that question is simply to collect data. But unless the data collection is designed to test specific hypotheses, the crucial evidence that would distinguish between competing hypotheses is often missing, so varying conclusions can be consistent with a single set of data. Furthermore, sometimes data collection is not done in a scientific manner but rather anecdotally. Anecdotes may, in fact, reveal important truths, but to be convinced of that, we need wide-ranging data that have been collected with the most scrupulously scientific methodology. We should keep this in mind as we proceed.

Some scholars have claimed that women and men in the United States talk differently in several ways. Let's consider six common and representative claims that I have come across in the literature:

1. Men interrupt women more than vice versa.
2. Men ignore the topics that women initiate in conversation.
3. Men do not give verbal recognition of the contributions women make to conversation.
4. Men use more curse words and coarse language than women.
5. Men use more nonstandard forms (such as "ain't") than women.
6. Men are more innovative, accepting language change more readily than women.

Students are often familiar with claims 1 through 4—or, if not familiar, tend to find them probable—but they may never have thought about the other claims and have no idea of whether or not they are probable. Claims 1 through 4 concern conversational behavior that the ordinary person is sensitized to. Many of us were taught as children that some of the behavior attributed to males in claims 1 through 4 is rude and shouldn't be done. Claims 5 and 6, on the other hand, concern conversational behavior that linguists are more likely to notice than the ordinary public. I include them because they are among the most important for anyone who cares about language change.

Consider the first three claims. How do they differ from the next three? That is, what aspect(s) of language are the first three claims about and what aspect(s) of language are the second three claims about? The first three involve interactive behavior in a conversation, whereas the last three involve individuals' speech patterns.

Try to imagine a conversation with someone who (1) interrupted you, (2) did not pay attention to the topics you introduced into the conversation, and (3) did not acknowledge your contributions to the conversation. Have you ever been in such conversations? Why did you stay in the conversation, if, in fact, you did? You may have stayed because the other person had some societal position of authority, perhaps your boss, your doctor, or your teacher. In that case, leaving might have had adverse consequences.

Indeed, the first three claims about men's versus women's speech have been challenged on the grounds that, in single-sex conversations, if one person has more power than the other person, these same characteristics of conversational behavior are found. In other words, the first three claims are, according to some scholars, really about power differences, not about sex differences—an example of why data collection needs to take into account a range of possible (and sensible) hypotheses. If your data on conversational behavior involves only mixed-sex conversations, you cannot know whether the characteristics you find follow from the sex differences or from other possible differences in conversation partners—other possible differences might manifest themselves in somewhat complex ways.

Here's an example of real conversation (recorded by one of my students in a class on oral and written language in the fall of 2001). The two speakers are discussing a novel.

N: It was funny.
T: It was really descriptive.
N: It was funny how um the cat switched bowls. He uh fell into the bowl and breathed in the milk into his ear. It was . . .

T: I liked that one.
N: Yeah.

T interrupted N and also ignored the topic of humor until N repeated and elaborated on it. These two speakers are middle school boys. They are the same age, and the conversation is taking place at T's house, which might give T an advantage; on the other hand, N is the guest, which might give him an advantage. T exhibits more male conversational behavior than N does, according to claims 1–3. But even in this snippet of conversation we can recognize that the language interaction is complex. When T ignored what N said about humor, N ignored what T said about descriptiveness. They both wanted to put forth their ideas but were ready to acknowledge the other when forced. Is this typical of same-sex conversations?

Here's another example (recorded by another student in that class):

J: Um, how was your camp?
S: It was good.
J: What did you do?
S: Um, lots of stuff. I did a basketball clinic. That was fun.
J: Yeah. Um.
S: What was your favorite part?
J: Um, I think everything was my favorite part.
S: What was your specific . . .
J: Did you do a lot of crafts?
S: Not too many. I made a mask.

J interrupts S and ignores S's unfinished but predictable question. These two speakers are sisters; J is nine and S is fifteen. J exhibits more male conversational behavior than S does, according to claims

1–3. Given the age difference, we might be surprised that J seems to behave like the more powerful of the two. But if you consider the dynamics of the conversation, S seems solicitous of J—just as a big sister might be when a six-year gap is involved. It is important to notice that this same-sex conversation is quite distinct in participant interaction from the preceding one.

These are just two examples, although my classes over the years have collected hundreds. Almost all of them present interesting complications for claims 1–3, suggesting that factors beyond gender are relevant—perhaps age, familial relationships, location of the conversation, and so on.

The last three claims, although about individuals' speech, still present tricky questions for the researcher. Consider number 4: Do the social relationships of the two members of a conversation affect the degree to which they curse? For example, if they are teenage siblings, the girl is older than the boy, and there is cursing, does the male still curse more than the female? Not in some of the conversations I've witnessed. If there's one adult male with three adult females in an office, one of the females is the boss of all the other people, and there is cursing, does the male still curse more than any of the females?

Even if we disregard the societal relationships of the people and consider only gender, some questions arise: Are women more likely to curse with other women than with men? Are men more likely to curse with other men than with women?

As far as I can tell, claims 4 and 5 are well documented, but exactly what they tell us about men versus women is unclear. The prevalence of coarse language among men (claim 4) is surely not evidence of any structural difference between the ways in which men and women talk or of any difference in brain structure between the two sexes. Rather, this difference most probably follows from expectations about the levels of politeness that men and women are expected to maintain in conversation. In other words, the difference is sociological and culture-bound, not physiological. The prevalence of nonstandard forms among men (claim 5) is also probably a purely sociological fact, in that nonstandard forms are more likely to be taken as less refined; women in our society are traditionally expected to speak in a more refined manner than men.

On the other hand, claim 6 is simply wrong. Women often apply new sound rules of certain types more aggressively than men, whereas men are more aggressive in applying new sound rules of other types. It appears that women's speech has a greater orientation toward prestige norms than men's speech does. In other words, women, more readily than men, adopt innovations that are considered to be high class or smart, using language to try to get ahead economically and socially.

All six claims, then, are more about sociological factors than linguistic ones. It is important, for example, that women do not always use certain tenses on verbs, have a different set of word stress rules than men, or always place a preposition as the second word of their utterances. These are hypothetical examples of the types of differences that could conceivably come up if men and women really had different linguistic systems—but such hypotheticals never do come up in English. The grammar (i.e., the linguistic description) of women's speech in English is identical, as far as I know, to the grammar of men's speech.

This is not to say that we don't associate certain grammatical patterns with gender, but gender roles are not the same as one's sex. For example, consider vocabulary use. "Lovely" or "divine" might be seen as feminine language. A more feminine man might easily use these words, however, whereas a more masculine woman might not. So, again, these differences are related to societal roles, not to sex. We cannot claim that the grammar of women's speech is different from that of men's.

The preceding example of vocabulary choice relates to the United States. In various other countries, examples of differences between what men and women say can come from other parts of the grammar. In Japanese, for example, there is a usage called the *o*-honorific that textbooks tell us only women say. This is not true, however. Feminine men, particularly gay men, sometimes use this form. So, again, the linguistic difference is one of sociological gender roles, not physiological sex.

The question of whether physiological sex is ever the true factor in speech differences between men and women needs to be approached carefully. It is impossible to learn whether sex or sociological role is the distinctive characteristic for a certain linguistic usage in societies that do not tolerate overt gender role crossing and in which the power of men over women is stable regardless of situation. Therefore, the place to look is in other societies, like that of the United States, in which gender role crossing is tolerated and/ or in which men can have power over women and vice versa, depending on the situation.

If you'd want to undertake a systematic study of a particular language phenomenon, with an eye toward whether physiological sex, gender roles, or power relationships are pertinent in its analysis, you have to control for as many of the potentially relevant factors as you can. For example, let's say that you observe a situation in which a man and a woman exhibit distinct linguistic behavior regarding the use of a given word X. Let's also say that the man in the situation was traditionally masculine and the woman was traditionally feminine. I'm going to call this pair a. You can then search for other instances of that (type of) situation, in which you find the following:

b. Two traditionally masculine men
c. Two traditionally feminine women
d. A feminine man and a traditionally masculine man
e. A feminine man and a traditionally feminine woman
f. Two feminine men
g. A feminine man and a masculine woman
h. Two masculine women

By varying the people in the ways stated above, you might be able to tease apart the influence of physiological effect (if any) from gender roles (if any). But you can only be sure of your results if you control for power relationships, so for each type of pair you will have to find situations like these:

a'. Both people have equal power over each other.
b'. One person has more power over the other.

Furthermore, you'll have to test for a variety of ways in which people can have unequal power, including differences in age, education, finances, authority, and race. You will even have to consider matters as ordinary as whether the conversation is taking place in a neutral environment or in one in which one of the speakers feels more comfortable.

It's a daunting business, and unavoidably so. Because sociological factors are many and varied, sociolinguistic studies have to use impeccable methodology if they are to have a chance of getting reliable results (results that can be duplicated or confirmed in other studies). Most sociolinguistic studies, for that reason, are of a large sampling of people and present significant statistical data on a wide range of sociological factors as they report language data.

The introduction to this book promised to help you recognize how to use your own knowledge of language to answer many of the common questions people have about language. But here I hope I have impressed on you the need for serious study before making generalizations. These two positions are not contradictory. If you know how to approach language data, you can recognize factors relevant to the issue at hand and see the sorts of questions that must be answered before conclusions can be counted on. In the case of language and gender issues, these questions are far too many and complex to be ignored.

Further Readings

Coates, J. 1993. *Women, men, and language.* New York: Longman.

Coates, J., and D. Cameron, eds. 1989. *Women in their speech communities.* New York: Longman.

Eckert, P. 1989. The whole woman: Sex and gender differences in variation. *Language Variation and Change*, 1: 245–67.

Hall, K., and M. Bucholtz, eds. 1995. *Gender articulated: Language and the socially constructed self.* New York: Routledge.

Labov, W. 1990. The intersection of sex and social class in the course of linguistic change. *Language Variation and Change*, 2: 205–54.

Lakoff, R. 1990. *Talking power: The politics of language in our lives.* New York: Basic Books.

McCay, S. L., and N. H. Hornberger, eds. 1996. *Sociolinguistics and language teaching.* New York: Cambridge University Press.

Tannen, D. 1990. *You just don't understand: Women and men in conversation.* New York: Ballantine.

Tannen, D., ed. 1993. *Gender and conversational interaction.* New York: Oxford University Press.

Thorae, B., C. Kramarae, and N. Henley, eds. 1992. *Language, gender and society.* Rowley, Mass.: Newbury House.

10 English spelling is hard, and it makes learning to read hard. Should we do anything about it?

Many children in the United States try for years to learn to read, and some never succeed. Educators talk about a fourth-grade reading level as a milestone in the process of achieving literacy. The accepted wisdom is that once students reach this level, they cross over from learning to read to reading to learn. So, on average, it would seem to take four years of schooling (not including kindergarten or pre-K education) to gain such proficiency. Gaining analogous levels of proficiency in writing skills takes even longer.

The stumbling blocks in achieving literacy in English are numerous, and many people have called for spelling reform. Instances of rebellion against traditional spelling are often used in advertising, like "lite" for "light." Chat rooms on the internet have something we can already call a tradition of simplified spellings. Indeed, they have a tradition of acronyms that exist only as spellings, such as "brb" for "be right back." Text messaging on cell phones is another situation in which simplified spelling is found. We can expect more as technology advances, and we can expect these simplified spellings to creep into other contexts. So here I want to ask whether spelling reform would be beneficial in all contexts, not just in these special ones in which the length of the message (as in the case of a cell phone) is an issue.

Let's look at some problems in the present spelling system. English is riddled with contrasts, such as these:

bait, wait (*not* *bate, *wate)
late, date (*not* *lait, *dait)

Here a given sound is spelled in two ways. (This particular sound is a diphthong, or what many grammar school teachers would call a long vowel.) A given sound is often spelled in multiple ways. For vowel sounds, simply identify rhyming words whose spelling differs on the rhymed portions of the words, as above. English has many such examples, some of which are homonyms (words with identical sounds, but different meanings) that are spelled differently, as in these:

beech, beach
bare, bear
sight, cite, site

There are just as many multiple spellings for consonant sounds. The initial sound in each of the paired words below is identical, but the initial letter of the words in the pairs differs:

celery, salt
flame, phlegm
judge, gesture

To complicate matters further, a given letter or series of letters can represent multiple sounds. Thus the initial letters in each of the paired words below is identical, but the words start with different sounds:

Consonants

celery, cool
sugar, salt
go, ginger

Vowels

oh, on
am, all
eat, ever

In addition, a given letter or series of letters can represent no sound at all:

*k*nee
wa*l*k
veg*e*table
temper*a*mental
requir*e* (*contrast to* choir)

As if homonyms weren't confusing enough, English also has homographs (words with identical spelling but different meanings), which sound different:

read (as in "Let's read") read (as in "I've read it")
lead (as in "Lead me"), lead (as in "Lead pipes break")

Examples like these enormously complicate the task of achieving literacy. It's no wonder American children (as well as children and adults anywhere who are learning to read English) take years to gain adequate skills in reading and even more years to produce reasonably accurate spelling.

Italian children have an easier task, because the correspondence between the way one pronounces a word in standard Italian and the way one spells that word is much closer to a one-to-one relationship than it is in English. The concept of a spelling bee in Italy would be ridiculous. (But the matter is complicated if the person who is learning to read does not have the standard pronunciation. I will return to this point below.)

Our spelling system may well be a culprit in illiteracy, which is a persistent and growing problem in the United States. Although it is difficult to measure illiteracy accurately, given that there's a continuum of skills to evaluate, a 1992 National Adult Literacy Survey funded by the National Center for Education Statistics of the federal government and conducted by the Educational Testing Service (of Princeton, N.J.) found that 21–23% of our overall population has only the lowest level of literacy (level 1). That rate is higher in the elderly (44–53% of adults sixty-five and over), a fact that might suggest that our younger population is doing better. However, the rate at level 1 is also higher in people with eight years of education or fewer (79%) and higher in people from certain ethnic groups (38–43% of African Americans, roughly 50% of the various types of Latino groups, and 30–36% of Asians). Moreover, people who scored in level 1 tended to be poor (44% were below the poverty line). Since the percentages of both minorities and the poor are also rising, it's no surprise that illiteracy rates are also rising.

Given the problems with English spelling and the fact that illiteracy has serious societal repercussions, one might propose a spelling reform along the following lines. Adopt a writing system (such as the Roman alphabet, the system English presently uses) in which each letter represents precisely one sound, make sure that the system has a unique symbol for every sound that occurs in the language, and revise the spelling of all words accordingly. With these changes, a new reader only has to learn the association between each symbol in the writing system and each sound in the language. Once that is learned, reading is easy.

Although this sounds like a good plan with many obvious advantages, it has serious problems. Let's say we're going to adopt this system. And, for the sake of expediency and effectiveness of presentation, I'm going to suppose that you have given my husband the privilege of deciding which writing system we will adopt. I know this is arbitrary, but as a linguist I would have chosen the International Phonetic Alphabet—the system that linguists worldwide use when transcribing human languages. If I did that, however, you would have a lot of difficulty in following the examples below. Instead, I can make the same points by using my husband's choice (most likely the same choice most readers would have made)—the Roman alphabet.

To start our discussion, I'll choose as an example a word that you might never have worried about spelling correctly because it seems so simple. However, the spelling reform we are considering here would affect every single word, no matter how simple it might seem. I'll spell a short word—one that begins with a single consonant sound, has a single vowel sound, and ends in a single consonant sound: "car." Because we must assign a unique sound to each letter of the alphabet and we must assign a unique letter of the alphabet to each sound, it really doesn't matter at the outset what any of these assignments are. For the sake of familiarity with the old spelling system, I decide that the new spelling of "car" is "car" (that is, identical to the old spelling).

Now, however, things get tricky. I have a friend who says the word differently from me. In her speech the word "car," spoken in isolation (i.e., spoken as just a single word utterance) does not end in a consonant but in a vowel. So if she were deciding the new spelling for that pronunciation, she would choose "ca."

Another friend pronounces this word in yet a third way. She not only has no final consonant but also has a vowel distinct from mine. She has the same vowel sound in "car" that she has in "cat." Let me arbitrarily decide to use the letter "e" for the vowel sound in "cat." So if this friend of mine were deciding the new spelling, she would choose "ce."

I'm very sorry to report to you that I have another friend who pronounces the word in a fourth way. Whereas I say "car" with a puff of air immediately after the first consonant, he does not. We have different pronunciations. If our spelling system is supposed to give enough information so that readers can pronounce every word in a unique way once they understand the correspondence between letters and sounds, my friend would have chosen a different spelling for "car"—one I won't even try to guess.

I won't try guessing because there is no letter of the Roman alphabet that English now uses (in the present spelling system) for the "c" sound of "car" that is not also used for my third friend's "c" sound. So the best bet here is to use some new letter. In fact, there are many more sounds in English than there are letters in the Roman alphabet. Consider the words "thigh" and "thy." The sequences of letters "th" is used for two different sounds in these words, and there is no single letter in the Roman alphabet that we use for either of these sounds. Such facts mean that we will have to augment the letters of the Roman alphabet with additional symbols in our new spelling if we are to maintain the goal of having a one-to-one correspondence between sounds and letters. Since I don't want to go into the question of what new symbols we might add, I will simply leave you with the recognition of that need.

Returning to our discussion of the varying pronunciations, we face a thorny question: Whose speech should I use to determine the new spelling of the word "car"? Although I've given only four pronunciations, there are many other possibilities even of very simple words like "car." You make use of that fact whenever you mimic an accent. If you are convinced that your own speech is standard, compare your own pronunciation of several words to those listed as preferred in a dictionary. Look up, for example the following words:

affluent   caught   dog   garage   pen   police

Language variation, especially when viewed in the context of spelling reform, brings us face to face with issues of standardization. If you accept my pronunciation of the word "car" as standard, my friends have what you might consider nonstandard pronunciations. The third friend's pronunciation may even seem un-American, despite the fact that he was born and raised in America and has been speaking English all his life. However, in the parts of the country where my friends come from (I have lived in Boston, and I grew up in Miami) and in their social class, their speech is standard. And, although my third friend's pronunciation is undoubtedly the influence of being raised by Cuban parents in a Cuban-American community, many of his friends have similar pronunciations, whether or not they happen to speak Spanish, which means his speech is quite standard for some of the circles he travels in.

There's no way around it: These four variations on the pronunciations of this one simple word are produced by native speakers of English. Consequently, there is no linguistic yardstick for spelling reform that would allow us to choose among them. (To understand that last claim, see chapter 7.)

In matters of choosing a standard, then, nonlinguistic factors will have to prevail. But the question is, What do we use? Geographic information probably comes to mind first, especially after the examples above, since most of us can easily recognize speech patterns from other areas.

We can begin by focusing on an area of high-density population as our geographic standard. There are many to choose from, but I'll choose Brooklyn because people often talk about a Brooklyn accent. How will the aspiring readers from Atlanta, with their southern accent, be aided in their quest for literacy if the words they read are spelled in a way consistent with the pronunciation of people from Brooklyn?

Even if proponents of spelling reform are not discouraged by that question, there are still other questions ahead. For one, which pronunciation of Brooklyn will we choose? Not every native speaker raised in Brooklyn speaks the same variety of English. We could choose on the basis of population density again and ask which socio-economic class is most prevalent: upper class, middle class, lower class, or one of the hybrids in between. No matter which class we choose, however, aspiring readers from the other classes will be at a disadvantage vis-à-vis spelling reform.

The matter of whose speech we select as standard (to use as the basis for spelling reform) is important because the final determination of a standard will have undeniable effects on the degree to which the spelling reform aids literacy, and it may have effects as well on the self-esteem of aspiring readers whose speech varies significantly from the chosen standard.

Nevertheless, let's assume that we somehow manage to overcome the difficulties presented by both geographic and socio-economic variation. Now another huge problem comes up when we consider all speakers of English, not just American ones. How will a child in some Welsh village fare if she tries to read an American newspaper that uses this spelling reform? What about a child from Perth, Australia: Churchill, Canada; Calcutta, India; or Johannesburg, South Africa? Children in all these places speak English, but they all have different pronunciations. Today, although there are British editions of some American works and vice versa, generally the spelling differences between the two editions are minor. People anywhere who speak English and are literate can read materials written in English, no matter who they were written by. If America instituted a spelling reform of the type we've been discussing, this would change. And if the other English-speaking countries instituted their own spelling reforms, they would surely not choose the same pronunciation that Americans would. Thus literature written in English in a spelling-reform world would be of varying accessibility to speakers of English, based on the particular variety of English they speak.

Let's pursue this issue of accessibility. Can you read Shakespeare? Can you read a first folio of *Romeo and Juliet*, for example, and understand it? Even if you've never tried to do this before, I expect that you can. There are different dates for this play (1591 and 1596–97), but it is clear that it is over 400 years old. Assuming that the people who determined standard spelling when printing first became widespread were not trying to confound us all (a normal assumption), we can conclude that English spelling in the late 1500s had a better correspondence to pronunciation than it does today. This means that if we were to hear the words as people in Shakespeare's time actually said them, we would have considerably more difficulty in understanding the play. Still, even though the pronunciation of English has changed drastically over time, the spelling in Shakespeare's originals is close enough to today's spelling that, with some work and strong motivation, not only scholars but also ordinary literate people have access to the folio editions of the plays.

Consider these famous lines from the second act:

> O Romeo, Romeo, wherefore art thou Romeo?
> 828: Denie thy Father and refuse thy name:
> 829: Or if thou wilt not, be but sworne to my Loue,
> 830: And Ile no longer be a Capulet.

A literate person in the new spelling-reform age—whom I will call a new reader—not knowing how to read the old spelling system, would pronounce the words in a way that is consistent with the new spelling. Let's look at line 828 (the line in which the spelling is closest to today's). The new reader wouldn't be reading the line in the way you read it right now, with your pronunciation. Instead, she'd see each letter as a symbol that has a unique sound because that's the way our new spelling-reform system is set up. The first word, "denie," would probably have three syllables because there are three vowel letters: "e," "i," and "e," and the first and last syllables would rhyme because they'd have the same vowel sound. This pronunciation is far from how one says the word today. The second word would start with two consonant sounds because "t" and "h" would each correspond to a single consonant sound. And if in our new spelling the "t" symbol corresponded to the initial sound in "to" and the "h" corresponded to the initial sound in "hat," the word "thy" would start with the consonant "t" followed by "h," a sequence of sounds that is not found at the start of syllables in English today. The new reader at this point would probably be quite unhappy. The sounds she would glean from the old spelling would cause serious difficulties in recognizing the words, and her appreciation of the play would be seriously compromised, to say the least.

One way to make Shakespeare accessible to the new reader, of course, is to teach her both the new and the old spelling. But, then, what has spelling reform gained us? The whole point was to make it easier to develope literacy skills. If everyone has to learn two spelling systems, it becomes harder. Nevertheless, let's assume we can deal with English literary tradition, and let's also say that we have wonderful new writers in this age of spelling reform.

Now jump ahead four centuries (i.e., as far forward in time as Shakespeare is behind us in time). People will be speaking English differently 400 years from now; this is definite because language changes. Although some language communities are more innovative in certain areas of grammar than others, language changes over time in every community. Perhaps speakers 400 years from now will have adopted spelling reform again. These readers of the second spelling reform, whom I'll call the newest readers of the newest spelling, will have the same trouble reading our texts today in new spelling as the new reader had reading Shakespeare in old spelling. That is, the newest reader, if he wants to read literature written in the new spelling, will have to learn new spelling as well as newest spelling. And if he wants to read Shakespeare, he'll have to learn old spelling, too. Literary traditions—as we look both ahead and behind—would be seriously threatened by spelling reform.

In sum, spelling reform would probably not enhance the literacy of most aspiring readers of English (especially if we think in worldwide terms), and it would cut today's speakers off from their literary traditions.

These problems are practical in nature, and in some ways they are more sociological problems than language problems per se. But some strictly language problems would arise from spelling reform as well. For example, consider sets of words like the following:

electric   electricity   electrician

The second instance of the letter "c" in the first word corresponds to the initial sound in "car"; in the second word, to the initial sound in "salt"; and in the third word, to the initial sound in "sugar." In the new spelling, these three separate consonant sounds would have to be spelled with three separate letters, thus obfuscating the fact that this particular consonant (no matter how it sounds in each of the three words) is part of the same word unit in all three examples. With our present spelling, however, that fact is obvious. In general, our present spelling tends to make many such connections apparent, and they would be lost with spelling reform. Moreover literacy might actually be impeded because recognizing connections between words helps us not only to guess at the meanings of unfamiliar words but also to appreciate the interrelatedness of our vocabulary.

A staunch proponent of spelling reform might question whether the theoretical problems I've raised actually cause problems. Languages that have a written form, unless it was adopted in very recent times, have experienced writing changes. So what's wrong with spelling reform in actual practice?

Typically, writing changes have come about gradually over time. Some of the oldest writing systems were ideographs—essentially pictures that stood for whole words. Chinese characters originated in this way, although through stylization over the centuries they are far from iconic today:

月 moon
木 tree
新 new

Character systems often change into another type of system, which is based on the sounds in the word. One kind is called a syllabary, in which each symbol represents a syllable of sound rather than a whole word. So a word that consists of one syllable is written with a single symbol, a word that consists of two syllables is written with two symbols, a word that consists of three syllables is written with three symbols, and so on. Cuneiform, the writing system of the ancient Sumerians, was a syllabary that developed from a character system. Neo-Assyrian was a later stage in the evolution of this writing system.

		Archaic Uruk ca. 3000	Presargonic Lagash, ca. 2400	Neo-Assyrian ca. 700
DU	'to go'			
UD₅	'goat'			
GUD	'bull'			

Modern Japanese has a mixed system. It has both characters and two different writing systems, which are similar to syllabaries but differ in that light syllables are represented by a single symbol (as in ordinary syllabaries) and heavy syllables are represented by two symbols. A light syllable ends in a single short vowel (which is the most common type of syllable in Japanese). All other syllables are heavy; that is, they contain a long vowel or a diphthong and/or end in one or more consonants. This type of writing system—based on syllable weight—is much more frequently found than are syllabaries.

わたし   I   (pronounced *watashi*, written here in the Japanese system called Hiragana)

フランス France (pronounced *Furansu*, written here in the Japanese system called Katakana)

The third major type of writing system is very familiar to you—alphabets. For several examples of different types of writing systems, visit the Web site http://www.omniglot.dabsol.co.uk/language/.

Over time, alphabets have prevailed, and for very good reasons. With a character system, every word is represented by a different symbol. In fact, some say you need to know around 4,000

Chinese characters in order to read a newspaper with adequate understanding. Think how much schooling it takes to learn 4,000 characters. With a syllabary system, every distinct syllable requires a symbol. With the three letters of the Roman alphabet—"a," "s," and "p." I can spell thirteen words of English, all of which consist of only a single syllable:

a, as, ass, asp
saps, spa, spas, sass
pa, pa's, pap, pass

(Please allow me the apostrophe in "pa's.") However, we would need thirteen different symbols to render these thirteen different syllables in a syllabary system.

Alphabets, then, are the most efficient writing systems in that the fewest number of symbols is needed to render all the words of a language. Consequently, when a language community with some other writing system comes into contact with a language community that uses an alphabet, often the alphabet is adopted, typically with some changes to deal with differences between the sound systems of the two languages. And with the spread of alphabetic writing systems comes literacy for the common people since they can become literate with many fewer years of schooling.

Sometimes countries have resisted such changes, however, for reasons that are nonlinguistic. In 1446, for example, a Korean committee appointed by the king introduced an alphabet called the *hangul*. The king's goal was to encourage literacy among the common people. After his death, the medieval mandarins of Korea banned this alphabet, precisely because they wanted to keep literacy from the common people. It wasn't until four centuries later that economic, political, and religious considerations revived *hangul*.

Indeed, religious considerations are often relevant to the ease with which linguistic communities accept writing system changes or the strength with which they resist them. Some scripts are associated with religious or cultural traditions, and as such are preserved. Arabic script is associated with Islam; Hebrew script with Judaism, the Roman alphabet with Catholicism and Protestantism; the Cyrillic alphabet with the Orthodox Church; and so on. When attempts are made to revise scripts with associations of such great importance, the controversies raised can be heated.

In 1991 the government of Azerbaijan, recently independent from the Soviet Union, decided to change the officially recognized script from Cyrillic to Roman (adding to our twenty-six letter alphabet to reach thirty-two letters). Since Russian is written in Cyrillic, this change was like a banner of independence and opened up an orthographic can of worms. Azerbaijan is a country with ties to Russia, Iran (which uses the Arabic alphabet), and Turkey (which uses the Roman alphabet). A decade later these three alphabets exist side by side, with the Azerbaijani language written in all three. The choice of which alphabet an individual uses has less (or maybe nothing) to do with the languages of Russian, Farsi, and Turkish and more to do with cultural and political ideology. That is, which country you orient yourself toward personally is relevant and more influential than linguistic considerations alone. Scholars argue over which is best. Many want Arabic to prevail because much of Azerbaijani's traditional literature is in Arabic and because many of the people are Muslim. Others see the Roman alphabet as an important economic and political tie to the West. And some see maintaining Cyrillic as a way to ease the transition from their Soviet past. The debate continues, and in the meantime both new and old readers—to say nothing of tourists—flounder.

In 1998 Germany adopted a spelling reform that in a few short years has led to such acrimony that some states within Germany have rejected it and the country is now in a state of orthographic civil disorder. What should publishers do? What should teachers do? And where is the child who is trying to learn to read?

Sudden writing changes by decree (as in Azerbaijan and Germany), rather than gradual writing changes by differences in needs and habits, are generally painful and rarely totally successful. Thus, a spelling reform of English has little chance of faring better. Certainly, the attempts of the American Philological Association, the British Spelling Reform Association, the (American) National Education Association, and the Simplified Spelling Board from the latter half of the 1800s through the first half of the 1900s met insuperable resistance.

Although I conclude that spelling reform is not a good idea, literacy rates in America are deplorable. We must do something about it—for without an education, the future of any individual is unpromising. Unfortunately, there is no quick fix. The whole idea of spelling reform is at first attractive, I believe, because it would be so convienient to have a quick remedy. Who doesn't feel sympathy for the new reader who is facing the regrettable spelling of words like "neighbor" and "phlegm"? But spelling reform will not help literacy in the long run.

The answers to our literacy problems will take work, but I, like many other educators, have one answer to offer: Read to children. Go into schools and volunteer your time. Show children that there is a reason to go through all the work of learning to read. Offer them the joy of good books. Start with the very young, but don't ignore teens or, for that matter, adults who are struggling with literacy. In my experience, it works.

162   Language in Society

Further Reading

Daniels, P., and W. Bright, eds. 1996. *The world's writing systems*. New York: Oxford University Press.

Diringer, D. 1948. *The alphabet: A key to the history of mankind*. New York: Philosophical Library.

Gaur, A. 1984. *A history of writing*. London: The British Library.

Web Sites

German language spelling reform. http://german.about.com/homework/german/library/weekly/aa092898.htm

Writing systems and society. http://home.vicnet.net.au/~ozideas/writsoc.htm

Frequently asked questions on the national assessment of adult literacy. http://nces.ed.gov/naal/faq/faq.asp#9

Spelling reform menu. http://pages.prodigy.net/aesir/rere.htm

A plan for the improvement of English spelling (by Mark Twain). http://www.geocities.com/Athens/Acropolis/2187/twain.html

The fight over German spelling. http://www.linguistlist.org/issues/9/9-1493.html

New alphabet disease? (About Azerbaijan.) http://www.theatlantic.com/issues/97jul/alphabet.htm

11
Should the United States adopt English
as the official language and overhaul
the educational system accordingly?

The English Only Movement (EOM) has among its goals an adoption of English as the official language of the United States. Because the EOM is a strong and vocal movement in many states, it is important to face this proposal. But to do so, we have to understand exactly what it means for a language to be "official." Then we can consider its effects on schools. While the following discussion concerns the situation in the United States, many countries today have linguistically pluralistic societies, so analogous issues arise elsewhere.

The two largest groups that support the EOM are the U.S. English Foundation and English First. The former, with a membership of over a million, wants (among other things) improved education in English for immigrants in order to enhance their economic opportunities. English First, with only a little over 150,000 members, wants (among other things) to have English declared the one and only official language of the United States.

The above-stated goal of the U.S. English Foundation—that of enhancing the economic opportunities of immigrants—when used as motivation for the EOM reveals the assumption that there is a cause-and-effect relation between what language a person is educated in and to what extent that person is economically stigmatized. Immigrants typically move into poor neighborhoods, and their children often attend underfunded schools. Underfunded schools, regardless of whether or not they teach only in English, tend to produce students who are less prepared for the job market. Without a way to pry apart the effect of underfunding from the effect of what language(s) a school teaches in, the cause-and-effect relation that the EOM assumes cannot be maintained.

If the EOM were successful and English became the only official language of the United States, all federal activities would take place exclusively in English. This would include anything pertaining to national elections, such as information on candidates and voting procedures, and all evidentiary and informational matter in a federal legal proceeding. Under our present laws, citizenship via naturalization does not require English literacy for people who have lived in the United States for twenty years or more or for people over the age of fifty. The impact on the federal legal rights of these naturalized citizens is obvious. Moreover, in the 1984 presidential election, 77% of the Spanish-speaking voters that needed bilingual Spanish-English ballots were born in the United States. The adoption of English as the official language, then, would affect the voting rights of many citizens. A change in voter turnout could also have drastic effects on the political climate of the country, thus touching the lives of all its citizens.

If states were to follow suit and adopt English as their official language, all state activities would take place exclusively in English, including all matters pertaining to departments of motor vehicles. Thus, we should review the stated goals of the EOM and ask ourselves how the inability to get a driver's license will enhance the economic opportunities of non-English speakers. I'm hoping to impress on you the discrepancy between the stated goals of the EOM and the probable outcomes, at least in the short term. You can go one by one through other privileges on the federal, state, and local levels to realize the impact of such a change both on individuals and on society as a whole.

Through the Voting Rights Act of 1965, the federal government took action to protect civil rights regardless of one's language. On August 11, 2000, President Clinton strengthened these efforts by signing an executive order directing federal agencies to "improve the language-accessibility of their programs" by December 11, 2000. The EOM works indirectly against the act of 1965 and directly against the act of 2000.

Does the EOM aim to rob some citizens of their civil rights, as well as other benefits? If we can judge from the publications and activities of the movement, the answer is no. (See www.usenglish. org/inc/official/about/why.asp). Instead, this unfortunate result is incidental to its main goals.

Rather, the EOM's primary target for reform is the educational system. So let's consider a crucial aspect of education: funding. It is possible that if English became the official language of the United States, only those schools that adopted English as their only language of instruction and business (excluding instruction in foreign language) would receive federal tax dollars; and in states that adopted English as the official language, it is possible that only those same schools would receive state tax dollars; and on it goes down, to the local tax level. Schools with a significant number of students who speak a language other than English and who decide to allow (or even encourage) bilingual education might be severely underfunded.

Because education is the target of the EOM and because the use of language in education is something linguistics can help us understand, I want to address at length the question of whether or not instruction totally in English, in all classes other than foreign language classes, would improve conditions in the United States. But, first, I will examine briefly what could be unstated motivations of the EOM.

One such motive might be patriotism, which could be expected to figure prominently, particularly since the acts of terrorism of September 11, 2001. Aside from language, several different ways in which culture related to family origins can be expressed include food (probably foremost) and then (in no particular order) religion, music, child-rearing habits, dancing, appreciation of certain types of art, decoration of home and self, and superstitions. Is there any necessary relationship between these things and a person's patriotism? Surely Americans must answer no. Americans value a multicultural society, which America has been since its inception. It is significant that there isn't any movement to reduce the types of food enjoyed in the United States, the different religions practiced, the styles and traditions of music produced and listened to, and so on. Why should language be singled out from other cultural habits?

This brings us to what could be a second unstated motivation of the EOM: a country in which everyone understands each other perfectly. At first glance it seems patently obvious that if everyone speaks a single language, miscommunications won't occur. A second glance reveals the error. Most divorces are not between people of different native languages, yet miscommunication is a commonly cited grievance between parting spouses. Also consider ordinary, daily situations—not ones like lovers' spats, which are highly charged emotionally and thus might be more susceptible to miscommunication. For example, I was peppering a sauce and my daughter said to me, "You can't add too much pepper." Now what did she mean? Was she warning me not to add any more pepper? Or was she encouraging me to make it spicey? The two readings of this sentence are contradictory. My daughter didn't intend to confound me, but she did.

Miscommunication is common, even among speakers who share a native language, and some would question whether or not perfect understanding is possible among humans. If two people do not have a rudimentary knowledge of a lingua franca, they will be hampered in communication. But a rudimentary knowledge is a far cry from a command of the language that enables a person to use it for all civil rights and educational matters.

Therefore, if either patriotism or the desire for a country in which everyone understands everyone else perfectly is a motive behind the EOM, it is misguided. Worse yet, the EOM might reinforce and exaggerate the very inequities it aims to correct.

Now it's time to face the major target of the EOM: language in education. Let's begin with a historical perspective. In colonial America, settlers came from England, of course, but many also came from other European countries, and some came from African countries. In addition, the indigenous people remained to varying degrees. Thus America has been a multilingual nation since its inception.

Bilingualism and trilingualism (and more) were common practices in the colonial classroom. By the end of the 1600s, bilingual English-German classrooms were found throughout the colonies, and instruction in both languages persisted through the mid-1800s.

Controversy over which languages should be used for instruction started at least as early as the American Revolution, when Benjamin Franklin, among others, worried that the use of German might weaken national unity and hinder government proceedings. Nevertheless, bilingual instruction continued in an atmosphere of general political detachment and tolerance.

Increased immigration of Germans in the mid- to late 1800s led to a newly energized debate over bilingual education. Again the debate centered mostly around whether people who spoke a language other than English could be good citizens, not whether instruction in a language other than English could be effective educational policy. With World War I, anti-German sentiments nearly kept German from being a possible language of instruction in the United States.

Just as English-German bilingualism was commonplace in the colonial classrooms, so was English-Spanish bilingualism in the California classrooms in the 1800s. However, the mass immigration of Mexicans, because of the gold rush, quickly led to anti-Mexican sentiments, and in 1855 California banned Spanish as a language of instruction. Later, changes in the laws allowed bilingual education to become more common again in the second half of the 1900s.

Now the EOM threatens to end such instruction and has already started its campaign in California. The passage in 1998 of Proposition 227 mandates changes in the educational system, one being that students with limited English proficiency (LEP) should be segregated from native English speakers and taught almost exclusively in English before being moved into regular classes. The term for this practice is "sheltered English immersion." The proponents of P227 claimed that this kind of immersion is more effective in teaching English language skills than simply placing LEP students in curricula designed for native English speakers—what can be called submersion—and more effective than bilingual classrooms.

As of this writing, it's too early to tell if P227 has achieved this goal. Immersion programs are not new, and studies of similar attempts in the past show that it takes several years before their effectiveness can be accurately assessed. Past programs have not proved successful over the long term (www.lsadc.org/kegl.html). The EOM widely publicizes the fact that the test scores of LEP students in California have gone up. What EOM does not publicize, though, is the fact that the test scores of all California students have gone up. Such an across-the-board effect cannot, then, be attributed to P227.

Some facts, however, are relevant in finding the best educational system for a multilingual society. For one, the EOM is right: Submersion doesn't work well. Immigrants in the early 1900s who were thrown into classrooms with native English speakers and who were not given any special linguistic aids did not do well academically. A 1911 study by the U.S. Immigration Service reported that 77% of Italian, 60% of Russian, and 51% of German immigrant children were a grade or more behind in school, as compared to 28% of native-born white children (www.aclu.org/library/pbp6. html). Native-born African-American children were not included in the study.

On the other hand, it is difficult to assess whether bilingual education in the United States has fared any better. Studies of the progress of LEP students mix data about children in English as a Second Language (ESL) programs with data about children in true bilingual programs. The ESL programs offer special instruction in English language skills but often place the children in regular classrooms for the rest of their studies. These are, then, submersion programs with English language instruction on the side. True bilingual programs offer instruction in both languages in alternating patterns.

Therefore, the real question is whether the immersion classroom or the bilingual classroom is a more effective approach to the education of children whose native language is not English. As far as I can see, no unproblematic study has yet been done. One thing we do know, though, is that children most easily learn to read and write in a language they know well. Furthermore, they master content material (science, math, history, etc.) better if the material is presented in a language they know well. Finally, good literacy skills in a first language are the best predictors of good literacy skills in a second. So children who begin their education in their native language are primed to learn well in a second language later in their education. These observations alone suggest that bilingual education will be more successful than immersion.

We might want to wait for the results of reliable studies before we make our own judgment here, but we cannot afford to wait. There is a lot of personal wealth behind the EOM, and it is funding drives for propositions similar to California's P227 in other states. So, based on our own experience, let's try to answer the question of whether an immersion or a bilingual classroom is preferable.

Pretend you are a small child who is entering school. You are handed a beautiful book. You open it up and see

αγαθὸζ ο αυθρωποζ

You might exclaim, "This is Greek to me! It's not even the Roman alphabet." Well, you're right. This is ancient Greek, and your reaction helps me to make an important point. If I gave you a passage written in the Roman alphabet, even if you didn't know the language, you'd know how to at least begin to pronounce the passage simply because you read English. Read this aloud:

Vi er her kun tre dage.

You are probably not pronouncing it exactly as a native speaker of that language (Danish) pronounces it, but you're probably not wildly off either. (This sentence means, "We're only here for three days.")

It's hard for us to simulate the experience of a child who is entering school because you already know what reading is. You know that the letters on the page correspond to sounds and that the sounds go together to form words. A child who is learning to read has to first learn that correspondence. It's important, then, to strip away whatever advantages you have over the immigrant child to really understand the task in front of him.

Here's our situation: We are American children whose native language is English. We have moved to some mythical land where people speak ancient Greek. We are now in school, in an immersion program. We have to master the writing system, and at the same time we have to master the new language. (Let's be grateful that we already know what reading entails.)

So with all that in mind, the line in front of us is, once more,

αγαθὸζ ο αυθρωποζ

What does it mean? How can we figure it out? The teacher points to the printed page and says something. Maybe it sounds something like:

ahgathozhoowthropoz

Lots of things are odd about these sounds. First, there's a higher pitch on the boldfaced sound (the first "o"), but that pitch height is not accompanied by extra loudness or length, unlike stress in English. Second, the "r" sound is trilled, unlike in English. Third, the vowels aren't exactly the same as English vowels.

We see the letters and we hear the sentence, but we don't know which sounds correspond to which letters on the page. (If we didn't know what reading was, we wouldn't even know that we're supposed to discern such a correspondence.) We don't know from the sounds where the word breaks are because the speech stream of an utterance simply doesn't give that information.

Maybe this teacher realizes that we are lost, and he pronounces the words again, slowly. What would you do if you were the teacher. Say the following English sentence in a casual way:

This is going to be interesting.

Now pretend you are a teacher who is trying to help a child learn to read. Say the sentence again, this time taking care to pronounce each written syllable in a way that is close to the spelling. Unless you are highly unusual, you pronounced "interesting" differently the second time, and probably your pronunciation of "going to be" was different as well.

Most likely our teacher of ancient Greek did the same—the first pronunciation would have been different from the second. He's trying to help the child, but he's giving the child two different pronunciations of the same letters on the page. His good intentions aren't making the child's job any easier. All the child can do is mimic, like a trained parrot.

The teacher moves on to the next sentence:

τὰ τοῦ αυθρώ που παιδία καλά

And on to the next, which I won't even write because by this point we, the immigrant children, are desperately seeking any source of help. Perhaps our teacher looks at us with annoyance, interpreting our wandering eyes as evidence that we aren't paying attention. We're starting out on the wrong foot. A teacher's early impression is not easily overcome. Plus, like other children, we are aware of how teachers view us. We wonder whether school is a nice place or not.

The reading lesson finally ends, and, being immigrants, we are sent to a special support class (as in the P227 model). Our special language teacher knows some English, although she doesn't sound much like we do. She looks at our reading book and says over and over again that the first sentence means "The man is good." When we look at her with blank faces, she realizes that we don't know what reading entails or even what the linguistic unit of a word is. So she explains.

Now we are more confused than ever. The English translation has four words, but the Greek has only three. Our special language teacher tells us that the Greek word for "is" doesn't have to be written, that this is just a difference between Greek and English.

We point to the first word and say, "The"; to the second, and say, "man"; to the third. But before we can speak, the special language teacher stops us. It seems that the first word means "good"; the second word means "the"; the third word means "man." She tells us that words can come in many orders in ancient Greek. So we try the order

ο ανθρωποζ αγαθόζ

The teacher smiles in approval. Now we try the order

ανθρωποζ ο αγαθόζ

The teacher stops smiling. This order is no good because the word for "the" must come before the word for "man"— because, she tells us, that's just how it is. I could go on, but you're probably already sick of this example, and the child you were pretending to be is probably sick of it, too.

The list of the things that child has to learn includes (1) the letters, (2) the correspondence between letters and sounds, (3) the linguistic notion of words, and (4) the Greek language—with its different sounds and different syntax. It's a daunting list.

Now face one more fact: the little immigrant children, the children we were pretending to be, are marched back to the regular classroom. They now face science, history, geography, math—all taught in Greek.

Certainly learning Greek is not confined to the classroom. The child picks up words on the playground and in the lunchroom, although many words that come up in the subjects studied in school do not come up in these other places. Certain words are restricted to academic settings—like "photosynthesis"—so all the children in the classroom are learning these words for the first time. The immigrant child is simply learning them in Greek rather than in English. But other classroom words are part of our ordinary vocabulary, like "country" (in a geography lesson), "liver" (in a science lesson), and so on. Here the immigrant child has to do more work than the other children because the others already know the Greek word. That is, immigrant children struggle with language acquisition on top of subject material for a long, long time—for years, in fact, because the task is huge.

Let's now pretend to be children in a bilingual English-Greek program, which is organized in the following way. Each bilingual classroom has two teachers. Both are bilingual, but one is English dominant (English is her native language) and one is Greek dominant. The teachers teach in their dominant language (one teaching in English, the other teaching in Greek), although they listen and respond to questions in either language. They take turns teaching the subjects: If one teaches math one day, the other will teach math the next. We, the children, hear all subjects in both languages, discuss all subjects in both languages, and read and write about all subjects in both languages. When the teacher teaches in our native language, we have just as much chance of learning as we would in a school in our native country, and we are still exposed to all the material in the other language that the child in the immersion program is exposed to.

Now let's pretend we are children who enter a differently organized bilingual English-Greek program. In this school, children
are taught all subjects in their native language through the fourth
grade, with the addition of intensive language courses in the other
language. Then, in fifth grade, they are put into classrooms that
use the model described in the preceding paragraph. This particular school then moves to a regular Greek program in the ninth grade.
Thus we children learn just as much as we would have learned in
our native country through the fourth grade, at which point our
literacy skills are well developed. Now we move into the fifth
grade, and our task is simply to learn the subject matter, not to
learn both a new language and a subject matter at the same time.
Then in ninth grade, we change to an all-Greek program, but our
skills in our native language are so good that we can keep reading it and writing in it for the rest of our lives. This model, unlike the first one, presents problems for students who are transferring
into the program, problems that we would expect to be more
severe the older the transfer students are. Its advantage, however,
is that it exploits the fact that children gain literacy in a second
language faster and more thoroughly if they already have literacy
in their first.

There are other models for bilingual programs, but I've given
just these two because the first is one I'm familiar with (my oldest
daughter attended such a school) and the second is the one I find
most promising. I have no hesitation in concluding that I would
be most likely to thrive in some variety of bilingual program rather
than in an immersion program.

There's no doubt that bilingual education is expensive. And
if the school has children from two dozen different languages, no
community could afford to fully implement either model for all of
them. However, many communities in the United States have a

large number of speakers from a single non-English language. These are the communities that perhaps cannot afford not to implement an effective bilingual program.

The main goal of the EOM—of overhauling our educational system—affects all of us. A society in which children of any particular group receive a deficient education and, possibly, a negative attitude toward education risks predictable consequences. This is true whether the children have immigrant parents, are of a particular race, or are simply poor. Americans pride themselves in protecting one of the finest parts of their national heritage—the right to an education. Repeatedly, they have interpreted that right to mean an equal education.

Further Reading

Ambert, A. N., ed. 1988. *Bilingual education and English as a second language: A research handbook, 1986–1988.* New York: Garland.

Baker, C., and S. P. Jones, eds. 1998. *Encyclopedia of bilingualism and bilingual education.* Clevedon, Eng.: Multilingual Matters.

Cenoz, J., and F. Genesee., eds. 1998. *Beyond bilingualism: Multilingualism and multilingual education.* Clevedon, Eng.: Multilingual Matters.

Cummins, J. 1989. *Empowering minority students.* Sacramento: California Association for Bilingual Education.

Dutcher, N., in collaboration with G. R. Tucker. 1994. *The use of first and second languages in education: A review of educational experience.* Washington, D.C.: World Bank, East Asia and the Pacific Region, Country Department III.

English First. 1993. Response to questions from Senator Alan K. Simpson. U.S. Senate Committee on the Judiciary. Voting rights act language assistance amendments of 1992 hearing, 26 February 1992, pp. 138–59. Washington, D.C.: U.S. Government Printing Office.

Enright, S., and M. McCloskey. 1988. *Integrating English: Developing English language and literacy in the multilingual classroom*. Reading, Mass.: Addison-Wesley.

Frederickson, J., ed. 1995. *Reclaiming our voices: Bilingual education critical pedagogy and praxis*. Ontario: California Association for Bilingual Education.

Freeman, Y., and D. Freeman. 1992. *Whole language for second language learners*. Portsmouth, N.H.: Heinemann.

Garcia, E. 1994. *Understanding and meeting the challenge of student cultural diversity*. Boston, Mass.: Houghton Mifflin.

Genesee, F. 1987. *Learning through two languages: Studies of immersion and bilingual education*. Cambridge, Mass.: Newbury House.

Genesee, F., ed. 1994. *Educating second language children: The whole child, the whole curriculum, the whole community*. Cambridge: Cambridge University Press.

Oakes, J. 1985. *Keeping track: How schools structure inequality*. New Haven, Conn.: Yale University Press.

Zuckerman, M. B. 1998. The facts of life in America. *U.S. News & World Report*, August 10, vol. 1, p. 68.

Web Sites

American Civil Liberties Union. 1996. Briefing paper number 6, English Only. http://www.aclu.org/library/pbp6.html

Blake, R. 2000. A summary of Proposition 227. http://llc-server-2.ucdavis.edu/zope/SLAI/unzsumm.htm

Boulet, J. Jr., J. 2000. Clinton's tower of babble. http://www.nationalreview.com/comment/comment082300b.shtml

Department of Health and Human Services. Ongoing. (Accessed April 2001.) Office for Civil Rights. Title VI of the Civil Rights Act of 1964; Policy guidance on the prohibition against national origin discrimination as it affects persons with limited English proficiency. Federal register, 65, no. 169 (30 August 2000): 52652. http://www.acf.dhhs.gov/programs/ofa/lepnotic.pdf

An extensive list of publications on bilingual education. http://www.cal.org/twi/BIB.htm There is an extensive list of publications regarding bilingual education here.

Hakuta, K. What legitimate inferences can be made from the 1999 release of SAT-9 scores with respect to the impact of Proposition 227 on the performance of LEP students? http://www.stanford.edu/~hakuta/SAT9/ and http://www.linguistlist.org/~ask-ling/bilingual-multilingual-children.html

Linguistic Society of America. Resolution: In opposition to the Unz/Tuchman California ballot initiative: "English language education for immigrant children." http://www.lsadc.org/Kegl.html

12

Does exposure to and use of offensive language harm children?

Many people think exposure to offensive language harms children, whereas censorship of children's language and literature does not. Because such censorship is on the rise in the United States, it's timely to consider its effects. And because so many truly thoughtful people are in favor of censorship, I believe it is my responsibility to present the other side of the debate.

Censorship of speech is often an attempt to control language change. When I was a child, for example, many words having to do with sexual reproduction were taboo; teachers would scold children (or do worse) for using them. The list of words I was not allowed to say included names of body parts, such as "penis" and "vagina," words that are used in classrooms today. (Many of these words have since lost their nasty connotations.) Efforts to censor language, for reasons of religion or political correctness or anything else, aim to control language change by putting certain words out of use. Censorship is definitely a linguistic matter.

I am particularly interested in this issue, however, because, as well as being a linguist, I am a fiction writer for children. In addition, I teach writing workshops to children and adults in schools and writing associations all over the United States. As a writer, the two biggest language misconceptions I deal with are these:

1. Some language is correct, but other language isn't—so the character in my book shouldn't say, "I swim good" but, instead, "I swim well."
2. Some language is dangerous and doesn't belong in children's books, especially not coming out of children's mouths.

The first type of comment often comes out the mouths of editors, sometimes otherwise brilliant editors. Typically, I cringe. To understand my reaction, read chapter 7. "I swim good" is perfectly grammatical for many speakers. It is the product of a grammar that allows adjectives to modify verbs and verb phrases. That same grammar produces sentences such as, "She works hard," which probably most native speakers of English can produce in their ordinary speech. That "I swim well" is also grammatical (though stilted for many) does not in any way call into question the grammaticality of "I swim good"; grammars generate an infinite number of sentences and multiple sentence types. In a very few people's speech, only adverbs can modify verbs and verb phrases (so they would not say, "She works hard"). In many other people's speech, indeed, in most Americans speech, adverbs as well as some adjectives can modify verbs and verb phrases (where people differ on the range of adjectives they allow). In still many other other people's speech, adverbs, but, more typically, adjectives can modify verbs and verb phrases (so they would prefer "They learn quick" to "They learn quickly"). Younger speakers are more predominant in the third group, a fact that suggests this is the present direction of language change regarding modification of verbs and verb phrases.

By far, the harder misconception to fight, however, is the second—censorship. What follows is a position statement against censorship, which relies in part on your having read earlier chapters in this book. It has the following form:

1. Language is a basic human need and, therefore, a basic human right. It's like eating or breathing. That right must be protected from censorship.
2. Language does not equal thought, so attempts to censor thought by censoring language are both misguided and bound to fail. And, I should mention, if language did equal thought, attempts to censor thought are disrespectful of the humanity of children. So if I was wrong and these attempts were not futile, they'd be vile in any case.
3. Language is a fundamental way of organizing the expression of our experiences, both external and internal. It is a way to give legitimacy to the spirit. It is, therefore, a creative faculty, an artistic faculty, and as such it should not be censored. Furthermore, talking and writing don't cost money, so they are artistic outlets available to every level of society, including our most powerless—our children. For this reason alone, the creative faculty of language should be ever more vigilantly protected.

Many of the chapters in this book give relevant arguments for the first point. I want to add that I support this right even when it comes to something as hideous as hate speech. Of course, hate speech that is likely to provoke imminent criminal acts is itself criminal and cannot be tolerated. But that's quite different from hate speech that is a simple statement of opinion. Indeed, it's the right to express opinions that the majority do not agree with—unpopular positions—that we must work the hardest to protect since all of us have the right not to listen if we choose.

Chapter 3 gives relevant arguments for the second point.

It is the third point that we have not yet addressed in any way. We need to look at the forces on both sides of the censorship line and the values of the art of literature. The misconception I hope to debunk is that use of or exposure to so-called offensive language or literature is harmful to children.

I will begin by presenting the area I expect the most resistance to: my ideas about children's language use. Many people take offense at various types of language, depending on sociological and personal factors. I take offense at language that smacks of social elitism but rarely at swearing. My mother took offense at both. My youngest son takes offense at neither. I don't object to people taking offense at certain language. But sometimes adults forbid children from using such language—even adults who use that language themselves— on the grounds that using it is harmful to children.

This is objectionable, not because it is hypocritical (though that is certainly objectionable in itself), but because, I believe, it is incorrect. Children have all kinds of thoughts and feelings, and we, as adults who care about them, need to know what they are think- ing if they want to tell us. If we object to how a child expresses himself, that child might not talk about the matter at all, which would be truly harmful indeed.

But even if the child accepts our language censorship guide- lines, he might be thinking precisely the offensive thought behind the word. That is, by controlling the word, it does not follow that we control the thought. Often adults offer children alternative words, veering them away from "damn" and toward "darn" or per- haps some idiosyncratically chosen or coined word. But the child who says "blinkity" to everyone he's angry at and who stamps his foot and wishes vile things would happen to his little brother may, in fact, have more violent and cruder thoughts then the child who says "asshole" when she lifts her defiant little chin to her father. If you truly believe that saying "damn" harms a child, how can you not believe that saying "darn" or "blinkity" harms the child? This sort of censorship is out of focus. It's as absurd as concluding that a child is well behaved and happy because she's wearing clean, pretty clothes. We should encourage our children to express their thoughts and feelings to us in whatever ways are natural to them if we want to help them through the growing-up process.

Let's now turn to the issue of censorship in literature. Let me give you some telling facts about how important this question is to the American public.

- The November/December 2000 bulletin of the Society of Children's Book Writers and Illustrators included the article "Banned Books: The Case for Getting Involved."
- The fall 2000 bulletin of the Authors Guild included the articles "Know It When You See It? You Can Still See It on the Internet" and "Celebrate Banned Books."
- Volume 33, no. 3 (December 2000) of the journal of the Associated Writing Programs (AWP) included *The Writer's Chronicle*, "Self-Censorship & the Alternatives."

I subscribe to all three publications. In the fall of 2000, I was preparing for a presentation on censorship for the winter meeting of the Linguistic Society of America. Given these publications, I didn't have to leave my home at all to do my research; instead, the research bombarded me. Censorship is a major battle, and it is being fought right now.

I was a speaker at the annual meeting of the National Council of Teachers of English (NCTE) in November 2000, and I received an issue of their publication. *The Alan Review*. Volumn 27 no. 3 (spring/summer 2000) included two relevant articles: "Creating a

Censorship Simulation" and "Middle Schoolers and the Right to Read." Professor Robert Small of Radford University in Virginia was cited in both articles. I wrote to him, and he sent me a thick packet of articles on censorship, as well as *The Alan Review*, 20, no. 2 (1993), which is entirely devoted to censorship.

I learned from these materials that the number of censorship episodes chronicled by the People for the American Way (PFAW, Norman Lear's nonprofit activist organization) was seven times greater in 1996–97 than it was in 1988–89, the numbers increasing each year. The PFAW discontinued publication of this valuable yearly record, so I do not know what has happened since—but I'm not sanguine. In 1999–2000, 152 challenges to books were filed in Texas schools alone (Texas is the most frequent site of such challenges), and 42 banning incidents resulted (catalogued in the report of the American Civil Liberties Union of Texas, September 2000). In these censorship proceedings, the dozen top complaints about books were the following:

1. Offensive language, the most cited complaint (24%)
2. Explicit sexual descriptions, the next most cited complaint (23%)
3. Incidents of violence or brutality, including rape (13%)
4. Disparagement of family values (8%)
5. Treatment of satanism, the occult, or witchcraft (8%)
6. "New age," antireligious stories (7%)
7. Examples of racism (5%)
8. Examples of substance abuse (4%)
9. Materials that include depressing, morbid topics (3%)
10. Attacks on patriotism or established authority (2.75%)
11. Texts that include antifeminism or sexism (1%)
12. Derogatory images of the handicapped (0.47%)

When a book is challenged, an imposing and growing number of school principals and superintendants around the country cave in by taking it out of the libraries. The biggest target is elementary school, whose children are least likely to be able to get to a public library on their own. So the censorship is most effective and destructive here.

When a book is removed from a library, editors in publishing houses notice. As they work on the manuscripts in progress, they ask authors to make revisions less for artistic reasons than to avoid controversy. What winds up in the child's hands is sanitized.

Worse, the marketing division of the publishing house is alarmed, so publishing houses self-censor to the point of not taking a chance on a book that has literary merit. (See the AWP article mentioned above.) Unpublished works are lost forever.

Worse still, creative writing teachers often warn their students about censorship and sometimes even censor their students' work themselves. Joyce Greenberg Lott writes about this dilemma from the point of view of a successful writing teacher in The Writer's Chronicle, 33, no. 4 (February 2001). Most horrible of all, writers listen. When a book like Snow Falling on Cedars is banned, writers shrink inside and put projects on ice.

The problem is so big that there is a National Coalition against Censorship, formed in the 1990s, which produces the quarterly Censorship News. The American Library Association (ALA) has an Intellectual Freedom Committee, which publishes the bimonthly Newsletter on Intellectual Freedom and sponsors an annual Banned Books Week, in which everyone is urged to check out one of the books on the list of 100 books most often banned. The ALA publishes this list. The NCTE has a Standing Committee Against Censorship, which publishes the pamphlet "The Students' Right to Read," and its major periodicals often dedicate issues to censorship. The International Reading Association (IRA) has a Committee on Intellectual Freedom and, with NCTE, produced the anticensorship pamphlet "Common Ground." There is a Freedom to Read Foundation and the People for the American Way (mentioned above), so the anticensorship groups are gathering.

It is not clear, however, whether they can hold ground. The foes are multiple and powerful, including the Christian Coalition, the Family Research Council, the Eagle Forum, and many others. Support from such groups led to the Communications Decency Act (CDA), which was passed in 1996, some portions of which were ruled unconstitutional by the U.S. Supreme Court. Immediately after the Supreme Court ruled against the CDA, Congress passed the Child Online Privacy Protection Act (COPPA), which requires Internet publishers to ensure that minors are barred from accessing material deemed to be "harmful" to them according to "contemporary community standards." Because web publishers are unable to restrict access to their pages by geographical locale, COPA effectively forces them to abide by the standards of the most restrictive and conservative communities in the country. Furthermore, people who use these filters have no way of knowing exactly what pages will be blocked.

In a study conducted in 2000, a thousand randomly chosen website addresses in the dot-com domain were submitted to the SurfWatch filter. Of the sites this filter blocked as sexually explicit, a team of evaluators found four out of five misclassified. The filter blocked the sites of a storage company in California, a limosine service in Maryland, and an antiques dealer in Wales. In another study that year, the first fifty urls in the dot-edu domain that were blocked by Symantec Corporation's I-Gear filter included at least three out of four sites that had nothing to do with sex. One was in

Portugese about a milk pasteurization system, one consisted of sections from Edward Gibbon's *Decline and Fall of the Roman Empire*, and one was a passage in Latin from the *Confessions* of Saint Augustine (probably triggered by the presence of the Latin preposition *cum*, which means "with"). So the whole Internet filter proposal is a farce. But even if the technology could perform flawlessly, this sort of censorship is as problematic as any other. Moreover, systems deny access to adults who either lack verification credentials (such as credit cards) or who don't want to identify themselves on the Internet. Other acts of censorship follow quickly in such a climate. The New York Regents Exam, for example, was criticized by free speech groups in 2002 for altering literacy passages in their reading exams to make them more politically correct (substituting "heck" for "hell" and the like). In sum, there are multiple efforts for censorship on multiple fronts, and the zeal for these efforts is so great that their clear harm is hardly noticed.

Most attempts to censor children's literature, in books or on the Internet, are, I believe, well intended. They are not meant to harm. Rather, they grow out of concern for children's well-being and the desire to control the world children encounter in ways that their supporters believe are beneficial—although there is little evidence that censorship will do that. There is, however, reason to believe that censorship harms children, denying them basic rights, just as much as it denies rights to adults.

One of the most powerful examples of this kind of harm is a book that was banned in the second half of the twentieth century— Harper Lee's *To Kill a Mockingbird*—because of an interracial romance. Many people who support censorship of books today would never include this book on a to-be-banned list. They would not want to be associated with that kind of racism. They would not want to teach their children that an interracial romance is wrong. Our societal values change, and what once seemed offensive is later seen as a right we want to protect.

Let's consider three types of subject matter that censorship efforts often target and learn how this censorship can harm children.

First, representations of a harsh world in which unpleasant things happen are often the target of censors, but children may actually need to encounter such representations. The *Censorship News* in the fall of 2000 said, "Angry weird songs often make adolescents feel less lonely and more connected to other kids." I believe from my personal experience and from observation that the same is true of stories. Many of us do not speak our most wicked thoughts or our most horrendous fears, which we, as adults, know are common. We know this partly from living so long and, for some of us, partly from reading. Reading gives us access to the innermost thoughts of the characters; it allows an intimacy that is often rare in real life. I was grateful as I read Jane Hamilton's *A Map of the World* to see my fears and paranoias come to life, and I remember this gratitude when I write for children. No one is more lonely than a child who thinks her thoughts are more wicked than anyone else's. Children don't have years of life experience to draw on when trying to put their thoughts and fears in perspective. They need to read about characters who have all the problems children worry about, and children do worry—middle-class, pampered, and protected children, as well as starving children in war-ravaged lands. They need to read about "depressing, morbid topics" (number 9 on the list of reasons for banning books) if only to be able to dispell their power.

Robert Cormier, the author of *The Chocolate War*, *I Am the Cheese*, and so many other excruciating books for young adults, said, "It is possible to be a peaceful man, to abhor violence, to love children and flowers and old Beatles songs, and still be aware of the contusions and abrasions this world inflicts on us. Not to write happy endings doesn't mean the writer doesn't believe in them. Literature should penetrate all the chambers of the human heart, even the dark ones" (quoted in Anita Silvey, *Children's Books and Their Creators*). Richard Peck, a winner of the highest prize that can be bestowed on children's books, the Newbery, at the August 2001 annual meeting of the Society of Children's Book Writers and Illustrators said, "Writers for children do not traffic in happy endings, because if we do, we risk leaving our readers defenseless."

Second, sexually explicit material is a target of censors, although again there is much evidence that children need to read such material. Sexually transmitted viruses and diseases, including HIV/AIDS, are rising among the young in the United States, and unwanted pregnancies occur more often here than in other industrialized countries, where comprehensive sex education is more readily available (see *Censorship News*—the newsletter of the National Coalition Against Censorship). Ignorance is a major culprit. Keeping sex out of children's reading contributes to ignorance, and thus to the rise of these diseases and pregnancies. Sex is almost invariably a controversial matter in children's literature because it is a controversial matter in our society. But as Nancy Garden, author of the prize-winning and popular book about a lesbian teen, *Annie on My Mind*, said at the November 2001 meeting of the Michigan Library Association, "If you remove what's controversial from the bookshelves, there isn't a lot left."

Third, violence is a target of censors, and often this type of censorship is justified on the grounds that exposure to representations of violence contributes to violent behavior. However, in September, 2000, Senator John McCain, chair of the Senate Commerce Committee, led hearings about the effects of the entertainment industry on children's welfare, hearings in response to a Federal Trade Commission's report earlier that month. McCain said, "Scholars and observers generally have agreed that exposure to violence in entertainment media alone does not cause a child to commit a violent act and that it is not the sole, or even necessarily the most important factor contributing to youth aggression, antisocial attitudes and violence." Richard Rhodes, author of *Why They Kill*, wrote in the *New York Times* on 17 September 2000, that "violence isn't learned from mock violence. There is good evidence—causal evidence, not correlational—that it's learned in personal violent encounters, beginning with the brutalization of children by their parents or peers. . . . Violence is on the decline in America, but if we want to reduce it even further, protecting children from real violence in their lives . . . is the place to begin."

What should we conclude? If I argue against censors by saying that reading a curse word cannot influence a child to curse, or reading material that questions the existence of a god cannot influence a child to question the existence of a god, I'm essentially claiming that the written word has little power. But the written word has tremendous power: What we read can open worlds. The very purpose of good literature is to disturb, to make us take a second look at previously held assumptions, to make us take a first look at things we haven't encountered. As a writer, I would stop writing if I didn't think my words disturbed.

My point, though, is that, if we keep a child from reading a curse word, we are in no way guaranteed that the child will not think exactly that curse; and there's certainly no evidence that teens who don't read have less sex than teens who do. But what we can be guaranteed of is that the child who is deprived of reading a scene through to its end; who is deprived of hearing the ring of real discourse in moments of terror, desperation, anger, or, indeed, of love and joy; and who is deprived of experiencing the thrills that the protagonists of stories feel—that is, the child who can read only censored material—loses the emotional insights and the truth of the story.

Tim O'Brien, the author of the magnificent novel *The Things They Carried*, says, "You can tell a true war story if it embarrasses you. If you don't care for obscenity, you don't care for the truth; if you don't care for the truth, watch how you vote. Send guys to war, they come home talking dirty."

There's no way around it: The cost of censorship is truth. When we censor the material available to our children, we lie to them. And lies to children are unforgivable. It's our job, yours and mine—as people who know that language does not equal thought and who recognize the values of language—to join the battle and disabuse our neighbors of their misconceptions about what censorship will and will not accomplish.

Works Cited

Brown, J., and E. Stephens, eds. 2000. Creating a censorship simulation. *The ALAN Review*, 27, no. 3: 27–30.

Celebrate banned books. 2000, Fall. *Authors Guild Bulletin*, p. 49.

Censorship News. 2000, Fall. National Coalition Against Censorship Newsletter, vol. 79.

Chen, A. 2000, Fall. Know it when you see it? You can still see it on the Internet. *Authors Guild Bulletin*, p. 11.

Cormier, R. 1991. *The chocolate war*. New York: Laureleaf Books.

———. *I am the cheese*. New York: Laureleaf Books.

Fore, A. 2002, Summer. N.Y. Regents exam examined. *Authors Guild Bulletin*, pp. 65 and 39.

Greenberg Lott, J. 2001, February. The yin and yang of teaching creative writing. *The Writer's Chronicle*, 33, no 4: 40–44.

Guterson, D. 1995. *Snow falling on cedars*. New York: Vintage Books.

Hamilton, J. 1999. *A map of the world*. New York: Anchor Books.

Krishnaswami, U. 2000, November-December. Banned books: The case for getting involved. *Society of Children's Book Writers and Illustrators Bulletin*, p. 9.

O'Brien, T. 1999. *The things they carried*, p. 69. New York: Broadway Books.

Rhodes, R. 2000. *Why they kill*. New York: Vintage Books.

Schiffrin, A. 2000. Self-censorship & the alternatives: The self-censorship of big publishers and their money. *The Writer's Chronicle*, 33, no. 3: 50–56.

Silvey, A. 1995. *Children's books and their creators*. Boston, Mass.: Houghton Mifflin.

Simmons, J. 2000. Middle schoolers and the right to read. *The ALAN Review*, 27, no. 3: 45–49.

Further Reading

Brown, J. 1994. *Preserving intellectual freedom: Fighting censorship in our schools*. Urbana, Ill: National Council of Teachers of English.

Davis, J., ed. 1979. *Dealing with censorship*. Urbana, Ill.: National Council of Teachers of English.

Journal of Youth Services in Libraries, 13, no. 2. 2000, Winter. Association for Library Service to Children.

Karolides, N., L. Burress, and J. Kean, eds. 1993. *Censored books: Critical viewpoints*. Metuchen, N.J.: Scarecrow Press.

Web Sites

Nunberg, G. The Internet filter farce. http://www.prospect.org/org-bin/printable.cgi

The 100 Most Frequently Challenged Books of 1990–1999. http://www.ala.org/alaorg/oif/top100bannedbooks.html

Index